The Supernatural in Yorkshire

by
Tom Cunniff

Dalesman Books
1985

The Dalesman Publishing Company Ltd.
Clapham, via Lancaster, LA2 8EB

First published 1985
© Tom Cunniff 1985

ISBN: 0 85206 848 4

DEDICATION:

Posthumously for my dear nephew,

Ian D. Cox, whom I respected and

admired beyond all words.

Printed by Galava Printing Company Limited, Nelson, Lancashire

Contents

Front cover drawing by **P. B. Rennison.**

Back cover photograph shows the stone spiral staircase descending to the hermitage beneath Pontefract General Infirmary—the skull in the recess was discovered in more recent years (see pages 48 and 49).

Title page drawing depicts Francis Griffiths and the Cottingley Fairies (see pages 23-28).

The Bargest, a mystical beast of huge proportions reported to have been seen over the years throughout many areas of the North. Why it appears is not fully understood, but it is generally regarded as a protective spirit rather than a harbinger of bad news [see pages 28 and 29].

Introduction

YORKSHIRE, this strange and beautiful county, has long had associations with the supernatural; from the days of our primitive ancestors and their mysterious rituals, to modern witchcraft cults. But the contents of this book are not intended to categorically prove, or in some instances disprove, the existence of this enigmatic contingency. That, I leave to the discernment of others. However, it is all too difficult to explain what is, more often than not, inexplicable. Why and how do ghosts appear? Did the witches of old really use 'magic'? Is there such an actual creature as the Bargest? Yet if these questions are unanswerable in the context of the 'supernatural', how else do we define them? Perhaps, to satisfy the hardened sceptic, we might suggest that these are the product of an over active imagination. But after talking with individuals who have personally experienced some of these weird, and oft-times wonderful, phenomenon at first hand, which you will be allowed to judge for yourselves—we must submit, if only in part, to the element of doubt.

Many case-histories have been included in the text, some old, some new, some even cross-referenced with similar cases from as far away as the United States of America—but always returning to Yorkshire. And although my home town, Pontefract, appears to receive an over-generous amount of exposure, this is not by way of my unyielding admiration for the place—but pertains to the findings and words of Colin Wilson. In his opinion, and worthy of having—he being one of the greatest living contemporaries in the field of parapsychology—Pontefract is unequivocally sited on unusual ground; in his own words; "haunted ground".

In the writing of this book, my curiosity for the subject has grown— I can only hope some of my fascination is conveyed to the reader.

Acknowledgements

During the compiling of this book, many people have provided me with invaluable information —far too many to give each one an individual mention—to these kind people I extend my heartiest thanks. To those who went to even greater pains on my behalf—like Richard Van Reel, curator of Pontefract Museum; the staff at Pontefract Lending Library whose patience never gave out; Mr Harold Turford (sadly, now deceased); Mrs Shirley MacLean, Managing Director of the Dropping Well Estate at Knaresborough—to these, I shall always be eternally grateful. Finally, an unconditional word of praise for the illustrator, Gary Nicholls, whose work has more than enhanced the finished product.

The back door of Alsop's House, now the Cross Keys Inn, Old Snydale. Although the name of the property has long since changed, the original door to which William Longthorne crawled, bleeding and close to death, is still very much intact [see pages 9-13].

1:   Ghosts and Hauntings, Past and Present

WHATEVER we think about the subject, ghosts have been with us for a very long time. I think I can safely talk in terms of thousands of years. The ancient Greeks were among the first to make any acknowledgement to such matters. But here in England, it wasn't until the late nineteenth century that psychic phenomena began to be looked upon seriously—with the founding of the Society for Psychical Research (S.P.R.).

So what exactly is a ghost, and why do they appear? Unfortunately, I can give no categorical answer. But there is one theory, offered by an eminent early parapsychologist, which has almost come to be accepted as the established precident to determine such outbursts—the psychometric hypothesis. But before I come to that theory, let me first elaborate by way of a brief summary upon a few of the prominent parapsychologists, or ghosts hunters, who have come to the fore. People like Sir Oliver Lodge, T.C. Lethbridge, Harry Price, and, in more recent years, Peter Underwood and Colin Wilson. At the same time, it doesn't always do to take too much high regard of a so called expert. For example, consider the exploits of Harry Price, a celebrated investigator of the paranormal between the 1930s and 1950s. For he was to take his role as such, way beyond the threshold of credibility, when towards the latter end of his career he led the most extraordinary expedition to the summit of the Brocken—where he attempted to transform a man into a goat. Needless-to-say, the experiment failed abysmally. Consequently he was discredited by the Boylie report in 1956, which branded him little more than a cheap charlatan.

But we here in Yorkshire are an unpretentious breed, and don't take kindly to derisory notions. Accordingly, we would have considered Mr Price and his endeavours to be of a crankish nature, long before the issuing of the Boylie Report.

Lethbridge was perhaps the most scientifically minded in my list of investigators. At the onset, he was convinced that this thing we call a ghost wasn't always necessarily the disembodied spirit of someone who has departed this life. Primarily, he concentrated on a theme concerning the concept of time—which no doubt inspired that remarkable Yorkshire author, J.B. Priestley, to some great extent.

Lethbridge recollects in one of his early books, **Ghost and Ghoul**, an incident which occurred to him while in a friend's room at Cambridge in 1922. As he was about to leave the room, a man entered. Quite naturally, he assumed this man to be a porter on an errand to deliver a message. The following day he happened to ask his friend whether or not he had seen the man in question. The friend was astonished at this, as far as he was concerned, no one had entered that room as Lethbridge left. It was only then, on reflection, that Lethbridge remembered the curious garments the mystery caller was wearing—hunting kit. There was no other conclusion to arrive at; he must have, in fact, seen a ghost.

Some time after, when Lethbridge had become Keeper of Anglo Saxon antiquities at Cambridge, he began to wonder at length about the interlude. This was where he fell upon his theory concerning time. Could it not be that the huntsman was a former student of Cambridge, and that, in all truth, he was not really dead and gone after all—but rather, he was sitting at home recalling halcyon days at his old college? In the midst of this the man's thoughts had been so intense that his psyche or spirit had somehow managed to materialise through the enigmatic dimension of time in the place where his thoughts were projected.

As interesting as it may appear, Lethbridge was soon to desert this train of thought in favour of a similar theory to that of Sir Oliver Lodge, i.e. the recording or previously mentioned 'psychometric hypothesis'. In more simpler terms, a theory which infers that objects and/or their surroundings are capable of recording certain types of events. In Lodge's own words, this is how he sums up the aforementioned hypothesis, taken from his book **Man and the Universe:**

Occasionally a person appears able to respond to stimuli embedded...among psycho-physical surroundings in a manner at present ill-understood and almost incredible as if strong emotions could be unconsciously recorded in matter, so that the deposit shall thereafter affect a sufficiently sensitive organism and cause similar emotions to reproduce themselves in his sub-consciousness in a manner analogous to the customary conscious interpretation of photographic or phonographic records, and indeed of pictures or music and artistic embodiment generally.

Take, for example, a haunted house...wherein some one room is the scene of a ghostly representation of some long past tragedy. On a psychometric hypothesis the original tragedy has been literally photographed on its material surroundings, nay, even on the ether itself, by reasons of the intensity of emotion felt by those who enacted it; and thenceforth in certain persons an hallucinatory effect is experienced corresponding to such an impression.

It is this theory that is made to account for the feeling one has on entering certain rooms, that there is an alien presence therein, though it is invisible and inaudible to mortal sense...

Lodge therefore implies that the individuals who are capable of picking up there 'hallucinatory effects' are merely witnesses to a parody being enacted before them. That the individual sees and hears the ghostly, dramatic reconstruction; but that the ghost, or, indeed, ghosts, are totally unaware of being observed by this third party.

Lethbridge finally hung his hat on the same peg. Only, he preferred to think that the medium which does the actual recording is some form of natural magnetic field, closely associated with water or a damp atmosphere. A process not unlike the principles of recording sound on oxidised tape.

According to the experts then, in a nutshell, a haunting is no more than a re-enactment of a violent tragedy, so horrific that its highly-charged emotional implications remain present on that same site for an interminable period after the initial event. And that certain atmospheric conditions, combined with a 'sensitive' observer, result in a tragedy being played back. This also seems to answer the reason why a ghost appears on a particular date—when the atmospheric conditions are on a par to those when the tragedy first took place.

But is this truly the case, that ghosts are nothing more than three-dimensional reflections? For if it is, how then would either Lethbridge, Lodge, or anyone for that matter, explain the alarming appearance and actions of the Phantom of Old Snydale?

This rather fascinating case-history dates back to 1965, when, during the month of October, at least three people were to witness a somewhat unforgettable experience. The location of these weird events? They all took place in the vicinity of Old Snydale, a small village between Normanton and Featherstone in West Yorkshire. The first to fall prey to this entity was a lady from Normanton, who, at the time, was a professional entertainer. On that fateful October night, she was returning from an engagement in Doncaster, her route taking her via the village in question.

As she approached the bad bend just before what used to be an old railway bridge, the brick supporting pillars of which still remained, she saw the lone figure of a man standing in the middle of the road. Nothing unusual in that you might think, as she did at the time. But as she drove towards this seemingly ordinary figure, she suddenly felt aware of a strange extraordinary coldness. A coldness that slowly began to creep up her legs until it finally engulfed the whole of her body.

Mindful of the time of night, the village proper being no more than a few hundred yards further on, instead of blaring on her car horn, she flashed the headlights as a warning gesture to the motionless pedestrian. Needless-to-say, the figure took no notice. As she came closer, a sense of fear began to grip her. For the man's face, neck and chest were coated in a mess of blood. What's more, his clothes looked strange, as if, somehow, they didn't belong. However, considering her predicament, she had little time to contemplate such matters, for she was now almost upon him.

Frantically, she swerved the car to the side of the road in order to miss him, although she was convinced that, even after her skilful manoeuvre, she had in fact run the man down. Yet curiously, there had been no sound of any impact.

Stopping, she opened the car door and half-climbed out of the drivers' seat, resting one foot on the ground to maintain her balance. She looked long and hard at the point in the road where the figure had previously been standing. But the man was nowhere to be seen. She tried calling out several times, her voice carrying on the still autumn air. There was no response.

That awful chillness she felt earlier was growing considerably worse. As if by some uncanny instinct, something told her to scramble back into the car, slam the door shut and drive away from that dreadful place with all haste. Call it a womans intuition, whatever, she reacted instantly to this compelling sensation of apparent foreboding.

But her encounter with the lone figure was not to end there. Two weeks later, she again had reason to use the same route. Only, this time, it wasn't so late. Perhaps there was also another quite hidden reason for her opting to use this quiet country road—what she had seen earlier, was it real, or a figment of her imagination?

Like an action replay, as she came around the bad bend before the site of the old railway bridge, low-and-behold, the figure was there yet again. The only difference on this occasion, he was not standing in the middle of the

9

road. Instead, he was now facing one of the supporting pillars of the old bridge, with his arms outstretched in front of him, as if taking his weight.

The headlights of the car were full on, and once more that terrible feeling came over her, that odd coldness that slowly progressed from her feet upwards. As she approached him, he turned his head towards her. It was almost as if he was expecting her. She felt her heart leap to her mouth for the blood stains were still present on his face, neck and chest. Then, as if he could actually sense her fear, in a strange agile movement, he sprang menacingly into the direct path of the car.

She had no time to brake for it all happened too quickly. It was also out of the question to try to swerve to miss him. If she had, she might have collided with the opposite supporting pillar of the bridge.

When the car hit the figure, as on the previous occasion, there was no sound of any impact. Quite simply, she had driven right through him. To say she was terrified would be an understatement; her nerves were in shreads, and her hands had broken out in a clammy cold sweat. This time, she didn't stop, but drove on with her foot down firm on the accelerator. During the remainder of that fearful journey, for the life of her, she dreaded looking through her rear view mirror—convinced that if she had, she would have seen that frightening vision seated in the back of the car. After this second incident, she was never to see the awesome spectre again. Now convinced that the figure was definitely not imaginary, she knew that at the same time it was not entirely real either—but a ghost. However, others were to be subjected to the phantom's disquieting presence; in particular, a frequent customer of the Cross Keys Inn, Old Snydale.

Each evening, Monday to Friday, as regular as clockwork, this man would call at the public house on his way home from work, his mode of transport then being a motorcycle and sidecar. His perfunctory habit of a pleasant drink with friends was to cease with an alarming suddenness.

It was almost eleven-o'clock when the customer left the warm confines of the pub. After two or three kick-starts, his motorcycle started up and he slowly pulled out of the car park and onto the main road. As he gradually began to pick up speed in the direction of Normanton, his shattering, unearthly experience was about to commence.

Suddenly, from nowhere, the motorcyclist felt two invisible, icy-cold hands slip round his waist, giving the impression that someone, or something was now tightly holding on to him. In startled precipitation, he looked behind to see if someone had indeed jumped onto the pillion seat. There was no one there, but the springs on the rear wheel had dipped considerably, as they would have had he been carrying a passenger. The temperature rapidly decreased and he felt himself encased in a cloud of freezing-like vapour. Panic stricken and rigid with fear, he drove on through the dimly lit village in mortal dread of stopping.

This remarkable feeling stayed with him until he reached the point where the road veers sharply to the right—a hazardous bend which leads onto the top of a hill, where the road sweeps down in a winding fashion to the outskirts of Snydale and Normanton. As the rider slowed his machine to negotiate the bend, the mysterious, invisible hands released their hold, and the temperature returned to normal.

10

Whatever it was that hitched a ride on his pillion seat had gone as quickly as it had arrived. His ordeal, understandably, was to leave a lasting impression; so much so that after his traumatic experience at the hands of the ghostly hiker he vowed he would never again use that same road after dark. The landlady of the Cross Keys assures me that after that time, the motorcyclist has strictly adhered to his vow.

The third and final witness, or, at least, the only other I personally know of, was a bus driver from Featherstone. That night, he was on the last run from Pontefract to Normanton via Old Snydale. His passengers were two women, who were seated at the very front of the bus. The vehicle itself was of the single-deck type, colloquially known as a 'one man' er'—operated entirely by the driver.

They were travelling along the lonely stretch of road which preceded the place where the lady in the first part of the story had her encounter. And as they were approximately half way along here, the driver noticed two small lights coming towards them from the opposite direction. It would be all very well to assume that these were merely the headlights of another vehicle— but the driver insists that these lights were of a variety he had never seen before.

Indeed, as the bus came into a closer proximity to them, the two lights converged into one, fairly large, brilliant orb shape. What is even more interesting is the fact that the driver is positive that, without any reasonable doubt, he could plainly see the figure of a man standing in the midst of the orb of light.

At this juncture, one of the passengers caught sight of the oncoming gleaming object through the windscreen. Unable to contain herself, she screamed out that they were about to crash. Momentarily, as the bus hit the light, a strong shockwave traversed down the vehicle's full length, and it almost felt as if they had hit a brick wall.

Understandably, the driver was badly shaken by all this. He brought the bus to a gentle halt, and with the engine still running, climbed out onto the road to inspect for any damage. Strangely, as he stepped out into the night air, the sensation that was prevalent to his two fellow victims—that awful biting coldness—was evidently present. In the meantime, the orb of light had now moved across one of the adjoining fields, where it eventually disappeared. There wasn't a single scratch to be seen on the bodywork of the bus, and yet the feeling of hitting something solid had been so real and intense.

It is difficult to ascertain just how this kind of thing will affect us. Some are capable of coping with it—others, as with the case of the bus driver, are not so fortunate. He became so distraught by it that he required medical attention. The driver ended his occupation as such that very night. Some time later, he took a job as a maintenance worker in the depot garage.

The controversy of the phantom finally came to a head. Stories were rife of the culprit being the ghost of a suicide who was alleged to have jumped from the old railway bridge in a desperate attempt to end it all. So loud became the public hue and cry that a member of the church was called in to investigate the growing problem. In the early part of 1966, with the aid of Bell, Book and Candle, the area was exorcised—I can only add that it must have done the trick, for nothing of this nature has been seen, felt, or heard there since.

But what of the perpetrator of these unusual attacks? Initially, I must admit I too was side-tracked by public opinion—the general consensus being that this thing was the ghost of an unfortunate suicide. According to conventional beliefs, such a victim's spirit is never allowed to rest in peace. The taking of one's own life used to be considered, and still is by some religious bodies, to be the greatest mortal sin we can ever commit. Yet no factual evidence came to bear in support of this ancient, though much believed fallacy. Local records did not reveal such a victim. However, something did come to light. And in this instance at any rate, it would appear to put paid to the 'psychometric hypothesis' of Lodge and Lethbridge.

I believe the identity of this ghostly intruder lay in the reporting of an odious crime, committed more than a century prior to these peculiar incidents, an account of which I found in a book entitled **Walks in Yorkshire—Wakefield and its Neighbourhood**, published by Banks in the latter part of the nineteenth-century:

The small footbridge that divides Ackton from Snydale was the scene of a cold blooded murder on the 17th October, 1828. A young man named William Longthorne, of Barmby Moor, near Pocklington, aged only eighteen years, left Wakefield at six-o'clock in the morning of that day, having walked from Aberford the day before and having lodged at Wrengate at night. He was on his way to Ferrybridge, where he expected work in the stables. In the morning he was accompanied by a man, also young, named William Mosey, son to a labourer at the gas works, and who lived at Wrengate.

Longthorne had met Mosey when on his way from Aberford and the latter caused Longthorne to be called up on the morning of the murder. The two were traced to Heath Common to Syndale, Longthorne being dressed in a brown frock coat and dark cord breeches, and carrying a bundle, and Mosey in a hairy cap, a blue striped smock and dirty cotton trousers. One woman described Mosey as a low, broad set, black looking man.

The two passed a man who was going the same road only a short distance before they reached Syndale, and this man, walking more slowly, went past the place of the murder shortly after it had been committed. He noticed blood on the trampled grass, but, seeing no person, suspected nothing.

The close where this happened was Dole Close and Longthorne was destined never to go beyond it, for when he and Mosey came into the lower part of it, Mosey knocked him down, got upon him, and cut his throat from ear to ear with a razor, dividing the windpipe and laying bare the carotid arteries, and then dragged him by the feet to the little beck and threw him in alive and bleeding and made off.

The cold water stopped the bleeding and Longthorne crept by the beck side and through the closes to the back door of Alsop's House, the Cross Keys Inn. Dr Buchannan, then of Loscoe, and a Pontefract surgeon were immediately sent for to attend him. Longthorne was unable to speak until his wound had been sewed up and then only badly "Yes" and "No"; but he made signs, and in the presence of Rev. Mr Hodgson of Normanton, wrote upon a slate a short statement of the attack, but, could not give Mosey's name.

He died in the forenoon of the following day. All that Mosey got from Longthorne was five shillings and a small bundle of clothing, but the latter he threw away after carrying it a short distance. The razor too was found in a field near the Dole Close. Longthorne had, however, other money upon him, namely, a sovereign, a guinea note, and eight shillings in silver. The coroner (Mr Thomas Lee) held an inquest, and the jury found a verdict of wilful murder against Mosey, and efforts were made to apprehend him, but failed of success. He was not brought to justice.

Longthorne's tombstone could be seen for many years in the parish churchyard at Normanton. I remember noticing it as a child—and the most prominent part of his epitaph: "... who was murdered most foul ..." But the stone has since deteriorated, and is now thought to be among the paving slabs in the path which runs around the perimeter of the church.

The evidence, then, to suggest that William Longthorne was indeed the phantom of Old Snydale is, to say the least, more than coincidental. The woman from Normanton who encountered a young man with a bloody face, neck and chest—Longthorne would have looked exactly like this after Mosey had slit his throat from ear to ear. The man with the motorcycle and sidecar: his invisible hitch-hiker mounted the pillion seat outside the Cross Keys Inn, the place where Longthorne breathed his last. Finally, the bus driver and the orb of light which floated off across a field: upon checking the directions of the witness, that same field leads to the site of the murder itself—Dole Close.

Any collusion on the part of these witnesses can also be ruled out, for they have never met. Even the date would seem to be significant. The 'happenings' all took place during the month of October—is it not strange that William Longthorne died on the 18th of October, 1828?

As for the 'psychometric hypothesis', here it does not fit the bill. The main objection is that where these people claim to have seen or felt the odd phenomena, it was always some two to three-hundred yards away from the actual site of the murder. And not one of them admits to have seen any kind of a parody being enacted before them. The real truth concerning this case, I'm afraid, will remain an anathema. But the ghost, whether it was Longthorne or not, must have appeared there for some reason.

By way of a vast contrast to the scientific approach of discerning the cause of these unnatural apparitions, there are a multitude of obscure factions who maintain that the true explanation lies elsewhere. From the 1880s to the 1930s, for some unknown reason, there was a strong upsurge of interest in the occult resulting in the birth of many aesthetically orientated societies. One of these in particular was the Golden Dawn Society—and one that Alister Crowley, the self-acclaimed Beast of Revelations, was to take a very integral part in. This group believed that life and death are a natural progression to our ultimate destiny—not unlike the reincarnation theory, but more in keeping with Kabalism, a mystic belief of ancient Jewish origination based on numeracy and the occult. It held that we live and die on more than one occasion, each time our spirit advancing to a higher plain of existence, but this line of continuity can be broken by a single, deft blow of fate. If, for example, I were to be murdered, just as Longthorne was, and likewise my assailant were not brought to justice, according to this tradition my spirit would remain on the same plain until I somehow managed to seek and find retribution.

Of course, this is purely conjecture. Personally, I prefer to think that the ghost was in search of restitution, as opposed to retribution; edging my bets, I'd say that it must have found what it was seeking in the service of exorcism.

At the same time, it is only fair to mention that no two hauntings are alike, and that the majority, more often than not, do tend to belong in the category of the recording theory. Equally, there are as many sightings of ghosts that have no apparent or logical explanation. Numerous interludes of this type have been reported on in the area; one place in particular is Methley, a picturesque village between Castleford and Leeds, where at least two farm houses have had more than their fair share of inexplicable, nocturnal goings on.

One striking house in the village doesn't have a single ghost but a trio of them. The property was built in the mid-seventeenth century—a beautiful, stone-constructed period residence, oozing with both charm and character. Apparently, the house was once a coaching inn, but reverted back to a dwelling some 150 years ago. The date inscribed above the door is 1642, a time when there was much unrest in the country and the ravages of civil war were about to be unleashed upon the district.

The lady who has lived in the house for more than twenty years told me of a chance meeting she had with her normally invisible joint occupants— three men, all dressed in clothes of a similar period, and having bovine features, with prominent, aquiline noses. They were rather small in stature, and appeared to her as very solid, material beings. She recounts that as she confronted them, the men looked as if they were getting up from some mundane activity—perhaps a game of cards—and that they even spoke to her in a kind and friendly manner. She assumes that she was privileged to see them because of her long standing sympathetic affinity with the old place. But in more recent times, she hears rather than sees the mysterious interlopers. There was a murder committed in the courtyard of the house on the 28th March 1670, although this mentions only one victim—not three. No other information has been unearthed about the property to shed further light on the haunting. As to the lady who owns the property, she wouldn't dream of having these 'olde worlde characters' exorcised.

On a parallel, not far from here, at Methley Park, is Home Farm, and this house is reported to have a haunted room. David Hodgson and his family have lived there for ten years or so—but they, to the contrary, have never witnessed anything of a 'visible' form.

It all began when Mr Hodgson's brother was moving into the area from Cambridge. On the first floor of the house is a wig room, what we today would refer to as a dressing room, situated on either side of which are two bedrooms. Mr Hodgson kindly offered his brother the use of one of these while undergoing the interminable upheavals of moving house.

Shortly after he had settled in the room, the brother was rudely awakened in the middle of the night by an odious, over-powering sensation. It was an indescribable feeling of pressure bearing down on his chest. An oppressive feeling, but other than that, indefinable. Not wishing to cause undue alarm, he kept mum about the sensation, but endeavoured to sleep thereafter with a light constantly burning.

Some months later, when the brother had long since moved to his new home, Mr and Mrs Hodgson decided to change bedrooms—to the one previously occupied by their guest, where Mr Hodgson was also subjected to the strange crushing sensation. It wasn't until he questioned his brother about his own stay in that room that he concluded it must be haunted. By what, or why, has never materialised.

Another such room exists at the Keep House of Pontefract Castle, a place referred to by Shakespeare as 'Bloody Pomfret', scene of many gory executions. A room which gives one of the house's residents the most tremendous feeling of foreboding on entering it—just as Lodge's theory suggests: '... that there is an alien presence therein, though it is invisible and inaudible to mortal sense...'

In the case of William Longthorne, there was an overwhelming degree of evidence to point the finger of suspicion in his direction—and it can be regarded as a ghost story in the literal sense. As to the two houses at Methley, and the Keep House of Pontefract Castle, although not circumstantial, they can also be regarded as a 'type' of supernatural incident. But there is one more sphere that I have not yet touched upon—that of the folk legend. This in turn will depict what I believe to be the three commonest aspects of ghosts and hauntings, and to the origins from which they derive—the factual, the inexplicable and the mythical.

Yorkshire is a colourful source of both folk legend and folk hero alike. As a child, I lived in a mining village in what used to be known as the West Riding. It was a settlement which sprang up from the supposed munificence of a wealthy coal baron by the name of Thomas Crossley and a place which lacked any real sense of history—that is, except for a tiny part of the area which did have some slight connections with a folk hero of sorts. The majority of the village was built in the 1890s, except for a small group of properties known, though not very endearingly, as the Old Cow Cottages. These were once a coaching inn and stables, refurbished later as dwellings for the benefit of the mining community. For a long, long time, my uncle and aunt lived in the largest of these cottages, the inn itself. Appropriately, it was in that house where I heard my very first ghostly tale.

It concerned the notorious highwayman, Dick Turpin, when on his legendary ride from London to York. This is how my aunt would relate the story: On cold winter evenings, when the wind was howling round the gable-end of the house, if one listened carefully, the sound of Turpin's bold steed could be heard pounding its way along the deserted lane outside. Its hooves thundered at the hard earth with the vengeance of the drums of battle. Once at the fork, the winged pegasus would flair its nostrils wide and scoff at the biting air. Steam would pour from those moist, black holes, spuming forth a stream of greyish vapour—then off once more into the night.

This may not be an exact word for word account of how she told the story, but by any standards it was enough to stir the imagination of every child, and I was to be no exception. In all honesty, however, my aunt had never seen this spectacular vision, nor even heard it for that matter, though perhaps subconsciously she could well have done. The story, I am convinced, grew from the supposition that Turpin had stayed at the inn when on his famous mounted marathon from London to York. Yet if the claims of many old inns up and down the country that the highwayman had also stayed there when on his ride are to be believed, it surely would have taken him the better part of six months to reach York! More poignantly, two years ago or thereabouts, it was revealed that the ride itself is questionable. Just as with the equally notorious Robin Hood, the folk-hero Turpin was found to be more myth than fact.

The point I am so obviously trying to stress is that these characters, along with their deed, have grown out of all proportion with the passing of time. And it must also be said that much of the real truth about them and their activities has been shrouded, even lost, in a veil of fantasy. A result, no doubt, of hero-worshippers and their enthusiastic admiration for anyone

15

who laid claim to robbing the rich of their money and goods, with the honourable intention of re-distributing the ill-gotten gains amongst the poor.

Stainmore is a wild region between Bowes, which used to be in Yorkshire but now comes under Durham County, and Brough in Westmorland. Here, the Rere Cross is to be found, standing solitary, dominantly defying many centuries of all weather conditions. Not far from this ancient boundary stone is an old, barn-like property; its lower rooms were once used as stabling quarters, while the upper floor provided living accommodation. It used to look, for-all-the-world, like a fortification with its strong, solid walls, barred windows and stone slabs for roofing tiles. Yet it was really an antiquated inn, the Spital House. But although its exterior appearance seemed drab and austere, warmth and comfort were always to be found inside. In this remote place, my favourite curious story was to take a firm foothold in the annals of folk legend—the infamous 'Hand of Glory'. A severed, mummified hand which was purported to have belonged to a dead criminal; an anonymous fellan who died on the gallows, his body left hanging to rot on the jibbet.

The hand was considered to be a magic talisman, which was passed down to the subsequent leaders of a rather cunning band of thieves and cut throats. A sort of macabre Yorkshire version of Ali Baba and his forty thieves. It was said that when a lighted candle was placed in the palm and fingers of this grotesque curio, combined with a secret curse then known only to the leader of the band, it would induce the robber's victims and household staff to fall into a deep and hypnotic sleep, thus enabling the thieves to go about their business of purloining the family treasures without fear of being disturbed. When the robbers had taken their fill, the curse was revoked, the candle extinguished—then off they would steel into the night, giving them several hours before the crime was detected.

When this motley band came to rob the Spital House, their plans were scuttled by a young, conscientious serving maid. It was very late, and outside the rain was lashing down in torrents. The landlord, by this time, was away to his bed, leaving the serving maid to clear up and prepare the establishment for the following day's trade. As she was busying herself, there came a feeble knock at the door. Knowing that the area was much used by footpads and their counterparts, her willingness to immediately admit the caller was understandably apprehensive. When she called out to ask who was there, a tremmering voice replied, saying she was a weary old woman and that she wished no more than to shelter for a while by the warm fire. Reluctantly, the serving maid opened the door just wide enough to reveal the shape of the old woman. She was dressed in a long black cloak, with a cowl pulled firmly over her head. Whimperingly, she pleaded to be let in, her clothes drenched by the constant downpour. Upon seeing the dishevelled sight, the maid agreed and led the old woman to a chair by the fireside. With her comfort in mind, the maid asked the old woman to take off her cloak, thinking to dry it for her. But the strange visitor would have none of it, causing her host to feel a might uneasy about the situation. So much so that, when she had concluded her duties, instead of going to her own bed, the maid settled down on a couch before the fire—telling the old woman that here, in fact, was where she slept.

In reality, the maid was only feigning sleep and kept a vigilant eye on the

16

stranger, her curiosity aroused even more by the old woman's footwear peeping from beneath the hem of her cloak. They looked undoubtedly like a pair of men's heavy riding boots, and not at all in keeping with the kind of shoes worn by old women.

Almost a full hour had elapsed, the house being enveloped in a deathly silence, when the leader of the band disclosed his true identity. Carefully, the maid watched him pull the cowl back from his head, whereupon he took the 'Hand of Glory' from a pouch and proceeded into its ritual. Placing a lighted candle in its palm and fingers, he chanted the curse:

> *Let those who rest more deeply sleep.*
> *Let those awake their vigil keep.*
> *Oh, Hand of Glory, shed thy light,*
> *Direct us to our spoil this night.*

He then stealthily crept over to the window and lifted the curtain to signal his contemporaries, saying:

> *Flash out thy flame, O skeleton hand,*
> *And guide the feet of our trusty band.*

The candle, which was previously burning normally, suddenly erupted into a brilliant flame. In the midst of all this jiggery-pokery, the maid saw her chance and cut a dash for the landlord's bedroom. Once there, she violently shook the slumbering inn keeper until he came out of his trance-like sleep and quickly imparted to him the devilish events she had seen take place. Immediately, the inn keeper reached for his gun, which he kept handy for just such an emergency—but the leader of the band must have heard his movements and ran out of the inn. The landlord, however, was not to be deterred. Opening the bedroom window, he fired at the fleeing figure, certain he had put a shot into him. No trace was ever found of the villain, but the infamous 'Hand of Glory', as you will find in a later chapter, turns up in the most unlikeliest of places.

The story is by no means factual, although it is certain to contain a grain of truth somewhere in its make-up. Eric Maple provides an explanation for this maleficent skulduggery in his book **Supernatural England:**

So generally accepted were the principles of magic in that county (Yorkshire) that during the nineteenth century burglars continued to use a ghoulish type of illumination known as a Hand of Glory or corpse candle when breaking into occupied premises. The candle which was manufactured from the fat of a body, taken from the gallows, was supposed to render the one who carried it invisible, and furthermore to send the occupants of the house into a hypnotic sleep in which they remained until after the intruder had departed. The candle quite literally lulled the householder's family and servants into the 'sleep of the dead'.

Fiction can become just as compelling as fact. I have listened patiently to dozens of yarns concerning headless horsemen, mysterious 'blue' or 'grey' ladies—but, in the main, I must conclude that the majority are concoctions of our own imagination, helped by such accounts as the 'Hand of Glory'. Particularly, I have found, when nature herself sets the scene—a full moon, a disturbing wind, clouds silently scudding across a darkened sky, causing fleeting shadows—in such circumstances, we almost will the unknown to happen. Inevitably, we see what we wish to see.

2:   Of Churches, Rectories and Clergymen

ALL too often, we believe the church to be an infallible deterrent against the supernatural. This concept may also be found in many of the best-selling fictitious horror stories—the church is presented as the ultimate weapon against the unknown. Bram Stoker's Count Dracula is a fair example of this. The demonic, blood-sucking vampire is frequently held at bay with a simple crucifix.

Yet for all that, surprisingly the church itself is by no means exempt from paranormal outbursts. On the contrary, some of the most unusual hauntings ever recorded took place in either churches or rectories, the most famous instance of all being Borley Rectory, commonly referred to as "the most haunted house in England".

The ghost of Borley reigned for many years. It was thought to be that of a young French nun, who constantly wore a facial expression of terrible agony. A sad, doleful creature with a distant, faraway look. The rectory was finally burned to the ground under highly mysterious circumstances in February 1939. At a seance held at the house in March prior to its raising, a spirit foretold the end of Borley and exactly how it would come about. As to the ghost, which also instigated poltergeist activities, there was a skeleton unearthed at the site—somewhere in the garden. After extensive pathological tests the remains proved to be of a young woman in her late teens to early twenties, the skull showing a deep-rooted abscess beneath one of the wisdom teeth. If 'these were the remains of the Borley ghost, the abscess would certainly explain the reason for her painful expression.

I don't quite recollect if exorcism was attempted at Borley—which leads me to another popular supposition: We matter-of-factly assume that no one, other than a member of the clergy, is capable of successfully administering this age old rite. But I do know of a long forgotten Yorkshire case history which took place at Carleton, near Pontefract, in the 1860s—whereby a singularly ordinary individual unwittingly exorcised the ghost of an unknown priest.

One Sunday evening, in the period of advent, a footman in the employ of a local wealthy family inadvertently found himself locked in the chapel of St. Michael the Archangel, a small Roman Catholic mission which has since been demolished. He was attending vespers at the time. Either he found the proceedings very boring, or he had had an extremely tiring day, for the footman accidentally fell asleep during the service.

It was near to midnight when he awoke, and naturally he was amazed when he realised the awkwardness of his position. But this astonishment was soon to turn to awe when he discovered, to his alarm, that he was not entirely alone. Standing before the altar, which was now draped for the service of the dead, was a priest whom he did not recognise. Dressed in black, the priest was evidently preparing to say mass. Presently, a deep booming voice broke the silence: "Is there anyone here to clerk this Mass?" Upon realising the priest's difficulty, and after the question being put a third time, the footman nervously replied: "I will clerk it".

On hearing these words, according to the footman, the priest's face beamed with joy; it somehow became transfigured, shining with such brilliance that the servant was barely able to gaze upon it. Shortly afterwards the mass being concluded, without the normal priestly benedictions apart from a faintly murmured word of thanks, the priest and funeral drapings disappeared. Darkness filled the chapel once more, but as to how the footman spent the rest of the night is not recorded. It is thought, however, that he was not released from the chapel until the following morning.

Understandably, he went straight back to the house and told his employers, the Hunts, along with the rest of the household staff, about his marvellous vision. There appears to have been no signs of scepticism, not a single unbeliever amongst them. The questions never arose as to whether he was drunk or sober, or that he might have seen the vision in a dream. The footman's story was immediately accepted with ready credence—but for one difficulty, the explanation. What did it all mean?

It was eventually agreed that the ghost belonged to a dead-and-gone priest who had neglectfully forgotten to say a requiem for the soul of one of his departed parishioners. This soul had been lying in purgatory, while the priest attempted by midnight appearings in the chapel to atone for this neglect in his spiritual duties, his constant endeavours being thwarted for the lack of a clerk. Unknown to the footman, when he responded to the Mass, the priest was relieved of his torment, allowing his weary, earth-bound spirit to rest in peace.

Exorcism, to easily explain it, is merely an extension of faith, although I am inclined to believe that the true connection between this and the church stems from the old moral homily that good will prevail against evil. The ghost characterises the aspect of evil, and, vice versa, the church represents goodness. But here, I must also issue the strongest of warnings. The ritual, as is illustrated in the Carleton story, may be carried out by any individual— but it must never be taken on lightly. If a tree falls in the middle of a forest, and no one is there to hear it, does it still make a noise? We presume it does— but we can never be positively sure. And it is rather like this when dealing with the out-of-the-ordinary. I need not go into lengthy details about the Ossett exorcism, but this emphasises my point perfectly. A man mercilessly killed his wife while under the impression that he was possessed by the devil. Throughout a whole night, a clergyman, together with a lay assistant, tried to drive the devil out of this demented, obviously disturbed young man. But they did not succeed in eradicating any evil; more to the point, they helped the man's instability to come to the fore. We already know the outcome—in the early hours of the next morning the young man murdered his wife. After the Ossett tragedy, the church made radical changes in its policies towards the administering of exorcism. The Wakefield coroner, Mr Phillip Gill, summed up the inquest in the following way on 25th April, 1975:

There are four lessons to be drawn from this inquest:

1. Exorcism, a recognised part of the church's ministry, can have dangers associated with it. Those who dabble in it are playing with fire.

2. Those who believe in and practice exorcism, must never allow their enthusiasm so to dominate their thoughts, as to exclude the possibility of there being a medical element in the situation with which they are concerned. Co-operation with the medical profession is at all times essential.

3. Exorcism must be administered only by those who are carefully trained in and properly suited to the work, and the haphazard participation by all and sundry—as the evidence indicated—must stop.

4. There is a danger too, in highly charged and emotional forms of religious experience. Many movements nowadays have tendencies in this direction. This man's involvement soon caused him to find himself out of his depth, and it was here that his mental derrangement started.

His wife's death was the result of an over-whelming tragedy, with criminal intentions on the part of her husband being entirely absent.

But it would seem, from an event at Emley Rectory, on the rolling hills above Huddersfield, that not all clergymen are so want to immediately dispose of wandering shades. Disturbing for them though it might have been, a vicar and his wife willingly put up with the antics of a noisy, periodical set of visitors—due, most probably, out of compassion for the misadventure of an earlier counterpart.

It all began one pleasant summer's day. The vicar's wife was in the sitting room when a heavy set of fire irons rattled and swung about wildly in the hearth—for no apparent reason. She looked at them, baffled by what she saw, unable to comprehend why the irons had suddenly taken to dancing this merry jig unaided by any physical means.

When her husband returned from his various duties she informed him of the odd occurrence. As a matter of interest, they were in the sitting room discussing this over afternoon tea. The room itself was situated at the end of a long, narrow stone-floored hallway with a solid, oak-panelled door leading into it—and this door was standing slightly ajar. As she began to tell him of what she had seen, a gust of icy-cold wind entered the room. The vicar naturally assumed that the front door had slipped its latch—automatically he went to reclose it but found the front door just as he had left it earlier, closed and secured. However, as he walked back to the sitting room, the narrow hallway felt as cold as the interior of a refrigerator.

Rejoining his wife at the tea table, their conversation had hardly managed to recommence when the fire irons began their noisy jig all over again. Unusual as this appeared, it was by no means the climax of the incident. For as they looked at each other in sheer bewilderment, they began to hear faint footsteps coming towards them from the hallway. Synchronised footsteps— slow, precise and in perfect unison. But as the sound built up to a crescendo, the advancing footsteps abruptly stopped outside the sitting room door. Some moments passed as they sat, apprehensively waiting for whatever it was to enter. But all remained silent—even the fire irons had gone quiet. Upon investigation, the hallway was completely empty and the temperature had returned to normal.

This was to happen on innumerable occasions, each time heralded by the rattling fire irons followed closely by the ghostly footsteps. It wasn't to be until some months later when the probable culprits were discovered. The house was built in the seventeenth century—a large, rambling place constructed in the church's heyday, when a vicar and his wife might have up to eighteen children and still have room for a small army of servants. It was one of the rectory's earliest incumbents who indirectly was the focus for these peculiar disturbances.

This earlier rector was a keen horseman and vigorously enjoyed the pastime of equestrianism to such an extent that it ultimately caused his death. Out exercising his favourite horse one morning, the animal was accidently spooked by something, making it rear and bolt with fright. The rector, caught off his guard, was heavily thrown to the ground, where he died almost instantly as a direct result of his injuries.

Later on in the same day a group of villagers happened to find his crumpled body by the waywide. Sombrely, they lifted him aloft and proceeded to carry his dishevelled remains to the rectory. His wife, it is said, was so overcome with grief that the shock almost killed her. She wailed and moaned bitterly as the bearers carried his corpse down the narrow hallway and laid him down in the sitting room—the same room where the more recent vicar and his wife saw the dancing fire irons and heard the ghostly footsteps. Thus, it wasn't the old rector himself they had heard but rather the sound of his corpse bearers. Today, even this distant echo from the past can no longer be experienced. For the old rectory was abandoned for a newer, more modern vicarage, its fate hanging in the balance so long it fell into a state of ill-repair and was consequently torn down. The last vicar and his wife to occupy the house let things well enough alone, perhaps looking upon it as a curious piece of the past—part and parcel of the house itself.

Now, both Borley and Emley have disappeared but one of the North's most renowned rectory's—apart from Haworth—is still very much intact thanks to careful restoration. Epworth, some 12 miles east of Doncaster, was the birthplace in 1703 of John Wesley, the founder of Methodism. His brother, Charles, who composed more than 6,000 hymns, was born there some four years later. In all, Samuel Wesley, their father, sired nineteen-children, ten of which survived. And it is Samuel Wesley we are more interested in, rather than his two much acclaimed sons.

I have already stressed the hidden dangers of exorcicm. But we now come to what is undeniably the worst force to be reckoned with—the poltergeist. It is destructive, noisy and, above all, unyielding. The word is of German origin meaning noisy-ghost. However, we are not entirely sure that these "things" are ghosts at all. They are inclined to evolve around unhappy teenagers and display remarkable feats of prestidigitation—acts of seemingly pure magic, levitation, disappearing tricks, strange noises, even the trans-porting of matter through solid barriers. It is now being considered that these uncanny "forces" are a product of the sub-conscious mind, activated by someone who is emotionally disturbed. In almost every case, when the point of concentration is removed (i.e. the unhappy teenager), the polter-geist ceases to perform. Similarly, in the event of someone suffering from this strange malady the church has proved to be ineffective. For where such sufferents have tried this in the past, it has only antagonised the situation. There is one small consolation; although it cannot be exorcised, the poltergeist lives a comparatively short existence, usually only a matter of months, before dying away altogether.

The Rev. Samuel Wesley's unwelcome visitor was definitely of the poltergeist gender. It lasted for several months, and any attempt to rid themselves of it proved inefficacious.

On 1st December, 1716, a maidservant, who was working in the dining room, heard the most deplorable moans as if someone was in the throws of death. Frightened by this, she told the family but they simply made light of it. That was, until several nights later, when almost the entire household was aroused by a tumultuous series of banging noises coming from the direction of the nursery or garret. The Rev. Samuel, to the contrary, heard nothing at all. Being superstitiously minded, the family declined to tell him of their experience on the grounds that he might misinterpret this as a warning of impending death—an ill-omen. They did eventually tell him of the incident, but he instantly dismissed the very idea and adamantly refused to believe in such things. That night, as if for his own personal benefit, he heard nine loud, consecutive knocks by his bedside.

From here on, the house was disrupted by many unusual noises. Footsteps could be heard pacing in empty rooms. The sound of someone running up and down stairs—and not only one set of footsteps—but several at a time. Another noise like the smashing of bottles, and many, many more too numerous to mention.

Mrs Wesley was in the nursery one day when she heard the now familiar knocking sounds. Trying out a simple experiment, she repeated the knocks. Amazingly, the polgergeist replied in the same manner—the sound appearing to come from the floorboards beneath her very feet. In a bid to locate the source of the noises, she looked under one of the beds—when a small animal, about the size of a badger, came running out. A member of the household staff, a manservant, saw the animal squatting by the side of the fire in the dining room. He said it looked like a white rabbit. Curiously, the white rabbit has always been considered a warning of death, particularly in the North of England. Naturally, they were afraid that this portent was announcing the untimely demise of the Rev. Samuel. But when this did not come about, it was decided that they must be dealing with witchcraft—something which the reverend had often preached against from the pulpit of his church.

The case has been concluded in various ways. One report, though only circumspect, has it that the Rev. Samuel physically wrestled with the poltergeist behind the locked doors of his study—and that he considered his opponent to be the devil himself. Mrs Wesley, on-the-other-hand, had her own views on the matter. She was convinced that the ghost, which the family nicknamed "Old Jeffrey", was that of her dead brother who, while working for the East India Company, mysteriously vanished without trace.

The old rectory at Epworth is now a Methodist retreat and is open to the public—best remembered as a shrine to John Wesley, as opposed to the site of a poltergeist attack. But apparently the entity has made a few brief reappearances over the years.

3:   Fairies and Demons

DURING the summer of 1917, while Europe was suffering interminably horrendous depravities, Cottingley in West Yorkshire was seeing the foundations of an incident which was to arouse puzzling interest the world over. That interest was to remain intact for generations to come. Its cause: two young girls, Elsie Wright, then aged sixteen, and her cousin, Francis Griffiths, aged eleven, who claimed to have photographed each other in the company of fairies in a nearby wooded grotto.

Elsie had already started to work for a living, as an artist for a local greetings card company. Francis, five years her junior, was still at school. As for Cottingley itself, it was then a tiny settlement on the outskirts of Bradford, typically constructed of blackish-grey, stone-built terraced houses —a mill area. Today Bradford has encroached on what little space there was around Cottingley, making the once village-type setting almost a borough. The Fairy Dell, as the grotto became later named, was no more than a hundred yards from Elsie's backdoor and was a place she and her cousin often frequented whenever the opportunity arose. It had a freshwater brook running through the middle of it—complete with waterfall and lush green vegetation on its banks—all in all, an ideal setting in which one would imagine fairies to exist.

Elsie's father, Arthur Wright, was an engineer by trade, but his true passion was amateur photography. It was his box camera the girls used to take the first photographs. On that eventful day, Arthur was developing a plate Elsie had earlier exposed while playing in the dell. As the negative began to clarify in the solution, he could hardly believe what he saw— Francis surrounded by what looked to be "little people". It showed her standing behind a bush, her right-hand propped underneath her chin, gazing quite composedly into the lens of the camera, while before her danced a quartet of tiny, perfectly formed, female figures wearing flimsy gossamer dresses and translucent butterfly-like wings on their backs. One of the figures, directly at Francis's elbow, appeared to be playing a set of panpipes. "What in heaven's name are they?" asked Arthur. "Fairies," his daughter nonchalantly replied. Being a prime example of a true Yorkshireman, a rather stolid character, he didn't try to pressure her into giving any other explanation but preferred to leave the situation as it was and wait for any further developments. One month later, those "developments" were unexpectedly to materialise. When Elsie inquired about the use of his camera a second time, he personally loaded the plate and willingly loaned her the instrument, curious to see if she would return with another unusual photograph. When Arthur developed this second plate his curiosity was more than satisfied. The main subject on this occasion was Elsie, sitting on a grassy embankment, holding out her hand to a gnome who looked to be about to step up on to her dress.

As I have already implied, Arthur was not the kind of man to be easily hoodwinked. Together with his wife, Polly, they decided to take a step they didn't entirely uphold with. But circumstances will out. They felt it necessary to search the girls' bedrooms. Perhaps they might find paper cut-outs or some similar paraphernalia—some **material** evidence that would offer a logical explanation. They found nothing of the sort.

When both girls were questioned, they emphatically denied any trickery—aggravating Arthur to some extent. As a way of chastising Elsie, he refused her the use of his camera ever again until she told him the truth. But the girls were equally adament—the photographs were not fakes, and there really were "fairies" living in the dell.

In the November of that year, Francis wrote a letter to a friend in South Africa, enclosing one of the photographs. She merely commented: "This is me with some fairies up the beck..." To Elsie and Francis, the event was not so startling. They treated it as an ordinary, everyday affair, with not the slightest hint of conspiracy or fraud on their part.

Two years later, after the primary commotion had died down, Mrs Wright attended a meeting of the Theosophical Society in Bradford. She was intrigued by the occult and openly confessed to have had experiences of astral projection (where the spirit is supposed to leave the body during sleep and travel to other plains). Uncannily, the talk for that evening was on the subject of fairies, looked upon by the society as nature or elemental spirits who occasionally appear to those gifted with "second sight". Understandably, she could not forego mentioning the photographs Elsie and Francis had taken depicting themselves amongst these wonderful little creatures. As a result, Arthur was kindly asked to quickly run off some prints from the negatives, which were duly handed round at the Theosophist's yearly conference held at Harrogate the following month. It was inevitable that the photographs would cause something of a sensation—to the point of one of them landing in the hands of Edward Gardner, president of the London branch of the society.

Now Gardner was no fool and was well acquainted with a weird assortment of faked occult photographs of ectoplasm and so forth. And on the face of what he saw, he was inclined to believe that the Cottingley examples were of a similar dubious nature. Through contacts within the society he managed to persuade Arthur Wright to send him the original negatives, anticipating that these would help him determine whether or not the technique of double-exposure had been employed. To his surprise, the negatives had not been tampered with. Furthermore, before he could be positively sure, he took advice from a professional photographer named Snelling. Under careful scrutiny, and with the aid of a powerful magnifying lens, Snelling proclaimed that they were simple, open-air exposures with no element of trickery involved. Moreover, the tiny figures had not been pre-painted onto sheets of glass nor were they made of a rigid substance like paper or card. According to his diagnosis, the figures had actually **moved**

A sylph-like tiny fairy offers Elsie Wright a harebell posy in the fairy dell at Cottingley.

during the taking of the pictures. On enlarging the prints, he was also able to state that the figures were not suspended on strings or wires. The negatives to him, quite frankly, were the genuine article.

While Gardner and Snelling were in the midst of all this, a very prestigious author of the period was to become entangled in what was rapidly evolving into the most sensational story of the decade. Sir Arthur Conan Doyle—he of Sherlock Holmes fame—had been asked by the **Strand Magazine** to write an article about fairies for their Christmas edition.

Hearing of the existence of the photographs, he immediately contacted Gardner and requested if it would be possible to see them. At their first meeting, it was soon agreed that they had been presented with a gift-horse that was too good to pass-up. Everything fitted in so neatly. A perfect setting, complete with waterfall, toadstools **and fairies**. But Gardner was an over-cautious man, so much so that he personally visited Cottingley to try and determine the character of Elsie and Francis for himself. Upon his arrival, Arthur and Polly Wright were amazed to discover that the experts were so strongly convinced of the genuineness of the photographs. But not so much as Gardner when he accompanied Elsie to the dell. For it was exactly as it appeared in the photos; all, that is, with the exclusion of the fairies themselves.

There was but one more decisive test to be made—a test that would offer conclusive proof—to Gardner at any rate. He purchased two identical cameras and a series of film plates which had been cleverly sealed by the company that produced them. (I understand the firm was Kodak). Armed with these, the girls were sent to take more photographs in the dell. The results were just as astounding. After the plates had been handed back to Gardner, and checked by the production company that the seals had not been broken or tampered with, the plates were processed. The first depicted a fairy offering a posy to Elsie, while another showed Francis with a fairy leaping across her face. But the third picture was by far the most interesting. At first glance it showed two fairies sitting in a small bush, with an odd-looking object suspended between them. Gardner, being a folklorist, and having amassed a wealth of knowledge on such matters, inferred that this was a "magnetic bath", a device weaved by fairies in drab weather conditions. Repeatedly, tedious efforts were made by the experts to disclaim the authenticity of this second batch of photographs. Again, they had little or no alternative but to conclude that the pictures **were** genuine.

In the Christmas of that year, Sir Arthur's article, together with the pictorial evidence, was published in the **Strand Magazine.** Its reception by the general public, although sensational, was met with heavy scepticism. The story was instantly labelled as a hoax. But in all sincerity, not a single photographic expert was able to repudiate the evidence presented.

Conan Doyle, to safeguard Elsie and Francis from unwanted publicity, carefully concealed their true identity when writing his article. But hardnosed journalists are not easily put off the scent when a good story is in the offing. One man, from the **Westminster Gazette,** proved himself a real news-hound. He wasn't slow in learning just who Sir Arthur's proteges really were. And it wasn't long before he arrived in Yorkshire to meet and talk with the girls at first hand. But his attempt to "break" the story—if this is what his true intentions were—ended in failure for he found the situation just as Sir Arthur had reported it.

Later, Conan Doyle himself was to waver in his belief of the phenomena. But he could not afford to evade the possibility that these were indeed pictures of "real fairies". Being as cautious as Gardner and his photographic experts, Conan Doyle called in Geoffrey Hodson, a professional in another field—a clairvoyant. Hodgson made the now popular pilgrimage to Cottingley, which hadn't seen so much activity in all its history. He also chatted with the girls and accompanied them to the fairy dell. But Hodson, was to go one further than anyone else—he claims he too saw the fairies. This must surely have caused a weighty impression on Sir Arthur and encouraged him to proceed with his book, **The Coming of the Fairies**, which was published in 1922. Public interest, however, had long since died away. The fairies had irrefutably come—and gone just as quickly.

In 1965, Peter Chambers, a journalist on the **Daily Express**, learned that Elsie was still very much alive and recently returned to Yorkshire after a long spell in India. The case being left wide open some fifty years earlier, he decided to interview her and ask outright if the photographs were in fact genuine. She would not commit herself either way, preferring to leave the open verdict as it was, the implication from this being that it was a confession of sorts. Again, six years later, Elsie was asked the same question by an interviewer on Nationwide on BBC television. Her answer remained the same. But she stressed that her father had nothing whatsoever to do with it— implying that something **had** been hidden.

Yet in various interviews which have taken place more recently, both Elsie and Francis vehemently proclaimed that the fairies did exist. Francis even admitted to still being able to see them, though not so clearly, out of the corner of her eye.

On 17th March, 1983 Elsie—now in her eighties— appeared on BBC television and announced that the whole episode was a fraud. The photographs **were** faked. But why, after countless opportunities in the past, has she waited until now to disclose the truth? Significantly, she is presently having her biography written by a local author—could this be disguised as an advantageous selling point? But Francis is still sticking to the original story. The fairies, according to her, were not fabricated.

The main contention against Elsie and Francis' claims has always been the photographs themselves. No one fully expected a "fairy" to look so conventional. To some, the most obvious clue to the mystery was Elsie's occupation—an artist. She could easily have made the figures and painted them, for she was skilled enough in her line of work. But if she did, what of Snelling's findings and all those other photographic experts? Snelling said the figures appeared to have moved while the plates were being exposed. But is this statement so remarkable? In almost all of the photographs, the fairies are standing on bushes or small trees— not exactly terra-firma. And if we take this observation one stage further, the faintest breeze would cause these trees or bushes to move and gently undulate. Therefore, did the figures themselves do the actual moving, or could it not have been the item upon which they were mounted? If a photograph is taken in moderately hot weather, when the print is blown up to its maximum enlargement there appears a strange heat haze around the subject. Equally, if there is the slightest movement during exposure, irrespective of climatic conditions and remembering that shutterspeeds would then be comparatively slower, that movement would be registered in a similar halo of haze. Could this then be how Snelling determined "movement" in the subjects? As to Gardner's "magnetic bath", it has often been compared to a girl's swimming costume hung out to dry. But then we must also take into account the evidence of Hodson, Conan Doyle's clairvoyant. After all, he also claims to have seen the Cottingley Fairies. Or was it more a case of him seeing what he wanted to see? The power of suggestion, combined with the right atmosphere (the dell being so typical of where we imagine fairies to live), as I have already mentioned in a previous chapter, can provide very convincing results. And it goes without saying that such a claim would have greatly enhanced his position as a clairvoyant. This may sound a little like derogation, but it is not intended as such. The implication is purely that it could be construed by some as an ulterior motive.

In my own view, with respect to the photographs, the figures do appear wooden and inanimate. And my opinion regarding the validity of the existence of the fairies was strongly biased long before Elsie's damning revelation. This was chiefly brought about by an in-depth interview of the two women, done by Walter Clapham of **Woman** magazine in 1975. Elsie partly let the cat out of the bag by mentioning a prank she and her cousin had pre-arranged out of contempt for "grown-ups". Francis, earlier on in the day the first photograph was taken, accidentally fell into the brook. Her clothes dripping wet and dirty, she tried to lie her way out of trouble, which only made matters worse. Consequently, she received a thoroughly good scolding for her efforts. Elsie, wanting to make amends for her cousin's downheartedness, borrowed her father's camera. And it was here, after evaluating a very pertinent question, that the plot was first conceived. If a child tells a lie, punishment is their reward. Yet grown-ups tell lies— what about Father Christmas, the Easter Bunny or even the Tooth-Fairy— do these not represent a form of lying? From their deliberations, the girls agreed to seek revenge, though in a rather intricate way. They would photograph fairies in the dell and let the grown-ups see them. And were they to accept these photographs in all earnestness, the girls had it in mind to retort: "But you know fairies don't really exist." However, their plan backfired, for the Wright's did not and would not believe in the existence of the fairies. But for Elsie and Francis the difficulty to own-up sooner was multiplied by the involvement of so many experts—all crying "genuine". After living with the fabrication for 66 years, Elsie finally broke her vigil of silence. Her reason: she said she did not want her grandchildren to grow up thinking their gran was a bit odd in the head. Francis may follow suit in due course.

After the destruction of the charismatic appearance of the Cottingley fairies, what of another supernatural entity, indigenous only to these parts— the Bargest? J.S. Fletcher, who began his literary career as a local historian —hailing from Darrington, near Pontefract—describes this mysterious beast in one of his early books, **Memories of a Spectator:**

I have never heard the people talk much of ghosts, but they had a firm belief in whatever it may have been that they called the Bargest, a strange, supernatural animal something like a hound, but bigger, the peculiar characteristics of which were that it made not the slightest noise in walking, and had eyes as big as saucers. I do not know if the Bargest was a good or an evil spirit, but there was an old woman, living a few years ago, who told me that when she worked at a certain farm the Bargest used to accompany her home every night in the dark months, never leaving her until she was safe within her own cottage.

From every account I have heard to date about this strange creature, it seems to have no other function than guardianship. It is considered neither as a portent of evil or an omen of good fortune. It simply accompanies certain people like an obedient watch-dog—"certain people" being the operative phrase. One of the famous Brontë sisters of Haworth, wrote of seeing the Bargest several times. It would silently walk with her across the desolate Yorkshire moors after dusk. From its description it is reminiscent of the guard dogs in the fairy-tale "The Tinder Box". Be that as it may, the very sighting of it, especially to the faint-hearted, must be quite an appalling ordeal. And although hardly ever heard of these days, it does tend to surface from time to time.

A night cook at Pontefract Infirmary used regularly to encounter the beast on her way home from work in the early hours of the morning—but only in the winter months, as Fletcher's analogy would appear to imply. It disturbed her so much that she took to altering her route home. Her evasive action didn't help, for the beast would suddenly appear behind her whichever way she went. She said that it towered above her, and that its head was enormous—yet it never made a single noise. This, to her, above all else, was the most frightening aspect of the thing. To say she had been befriended by a stray dog would be ridiculous; for which breed has huge, bright-yellow eyes? An even more surprising factor was that she didn't have to walk along the lonely country lanes to get home, but within the confines of the urban sprawl—the actual town limits.

A natural assumption, she thought this weird looking animal could not possibly be real. She began to wonder if it was a figment of her imagination. But the thought was soon dispelled one morning by a coal-miner on the early shift. She accidentally bumped into the man while taking one of her many detours—only to find that he also saw the monstrous hound. Not so long afterwards, Vic, her husband, acquired a small car—she agreed with the purchase of this, but only on the consideration that he picked her up from work every morning. Since this time, she has never seen the beast again. No one else at the hospital ever laid eyes on the creature—perhaps it is just as well.

A will-o'-the-wisp, a jack-o'-lantern, something belonging to phantasmagoria; not unlike fairies, the Bargest is a creature of mythical origination. Not a ghost of some long dead beast, but a phantasm, a visual illusion. But there is an acute difference between the two. Fairies are most commonly associated with the four elements—earth, wind, fire and water. They are, respectively, gnomes, sylphs, salamanders and nereids. They stem, most probably, from the days of the "old religion" or "wicca"—which we now call witchcraft. The Bargest, on the other hand, could well be Yorkshire's equivalent to the North American "Big Foot" or the Himalayan "Yetti". Alas, this elusive, fleeting creature—from whence it comes or where it goes— will remain yet another indefinable piece in the perplexing jigsaw puzzle of the supernatural.

4: Witches and their persecutors

TO ALL intents and purposes the medieval witch was a busy little beaver. Apparently, if she wasn't boiling down babies to make flying ointment, or casting harmful spells at all and sundry, she was unusually preoccupied with the kissing of the devil's rear-end. At least, this is how the witch is portrayed in books like the "Maleficarum"—the classic text book of the Inquisition. The witch was personified as totally evil—a malicious miscreant beyond all redemption. My reference to the witch in the feminine gender, I hasten to add, is not out of chauvinism, but it seems the majority of witches were of the female species. The witch was alleged to have had the power over life and death, a power that was invariably thought to have been channelled from the devil himself. In return, she paid the hefty price of losing her soul—a contractual bargain signed in her own blood. In reality, however, it is now known that this concept of the witch was more a contrivance of the church and its inquisitors. Hand in hand with Christianity came "old Nick", and the promise of eternal hell-fire and damnation for all those not adhering to its doctrines—resulting in excommunication and a bitterly painful death. At the same time, I do not wish to imply that "true-witchcraft" did not exist; conversely, my comments are intended to draw attention to what caused the death of countless victims in the name of righteous persecution.

Fortunately, Yorkshire never fully succumbed to the hysteria of the witch-craze in the seventeenth century. But, by the same token, the county did endure a sizeable quantity of trials for witchcraft during that same period:

Thence to Wentbrig, where vile wretches,
Hideous hags and odious witches,
Writhen Count'nance and mis-shapen__
Are by some foul Bugbeare taken:
These infernal seats inherit,
Who contact with such a spirit,
In a rock Want built her booth,
Where no creature dwells but sloth.

This rather strange old poem was regarded as a very evident allusion to one Yorkshire witch and her supposed practices, with a play on the words Want and Went. Wentbridge, a tiny hamlet on the then Great North Road, West Yorkshire, was said to have had many such witches who used to infest the woods that surrounded the area. Mary Pennell, the Yorkshire witch in question, was the most celebrated of them all. She led a roving kind of life, having a number of lean-to-shelters up and down the district, namely at Ledsham, Sheepate Woods and Norton. Working mischief wherever she

The cross-roads at the top of the Mary Pennell, near Castleford. Mrs G.E. Makin, of Beckfield Farm, Fairburn, near Pontefract, was travelling home one night in her car a few years ago when she saw a female form reflected in the headlights. It was seen to cross the road quite slowly, but had disappeared by the time the car reached the spot where the image appeared. Mrs Makin has not heard of anyone else seeing this 'ghost', although she has asked around the vicinity. She is firmly of the belief that she saw Mary Pennell that night—if only briefly.

went, she employed a kind of blackmail on people foolish enough to pay her in order to be unmolested. In other words, she was a little like a one woman maffia operation, either pay up—or be cursed. Understandably, she chose her victims with the utmost care; never intelligent people, but poor, less-witted individuals.

However, Mary's luck finally gave out. William Whitam, the squire of Ledstone, died after a long illness in 1593. It was popularly believed that Mary had bewitched him to death and sent him to the grave. But it seems strange that there was a lapse of some ten years after his death before she was brought to justice for her alleged infamy. It is a fact which has made many think she was no real witch after all, and that the accusation was disguised as a ruse to put an end to the old nuisance. In short, she had become a victim of her own stupidity—hoisted on her own petard. Or did this curious old woman have the capability to influence some darker power—not exactly the devil, but evil all the same?

On the 19th of May each year, in the ruins of Heath Old Hall, near Wakefield, the wandering shade of Mary, Lady Bolles has been seen by a number of people. One man in particular was Charlie Sylvester. Unfortunately now deceased, he was the caretaker of the hall for a good long time. Charlie's duties included a daily inspection of the empty property. He and his little dog, a terrier, would check the building for signs of vandalism and keep away any would-be trespassers. But one room in the house he would never dare enter. Even the dog would not cross the threshold of this chamber. Instead, its hackles would rise at the back of its neck—and no amount of

31

coaxing would get the dog past the doorway. Charlie always insisted that he saw Lady Bolles in that room on the anniversary of her haunting. He also said he saw her flitting down the steps at the front of the house wearing a green riding habit.

Lady Bolles was a relatively ordinary woman, apart from a few quirky idiosyncrasies that is. She died, at peace, in her own bed at the age of eighty on 5th May, 1622. Her funerary arrangements, however, left much to the imagination. In her will she drafted explicit instructions for her body to lay in state for a period of six weeks, during which time there was to be an air of festivity about the occasion. Orders were also left to purchase wine for the gentry and ale for the servants. Beasts were to be slaughtered then cooked in the great kitchens beneath the hall—the spectacle was to be remembered as a feast of unrivalled proportions. But the most unusual request she made I have purposely left until last. As was customary, her body would be buried in the parish church of the family seat, that being Ledsham. But her bowels, then considered to be the true centre of emotion and not the heart, were to be removed by the physician and interred in an unmarked plot in the parish churchyard of Kirkthorpe—about a mile from the hall.

Eccentric though she may have been, her death was due to natural causes, with no foul play to suggest the disturbance of her eternal rest. But unknown to Lady Bolles, her spirit had been cursed to roam abroad after her death some nineteen years previously—along with the rest of the Whitam family. Lady Bolles was none other than the daughter of William Whitam. When Mary Pennell was taken to the place of her execution after her trial and conviction at York Assizes in 1603, a place which still bears her name to this day—the Mary Pennel/Pannall Hill—she is purported to have cursed the whole Whitam line, saying none of them would rest until she had her revenge. And, on the face of it, in the case of Lady Bolles at any rate, it would appear that the curse was effective—what's more, her wanderings are not only confined to the ruins on the Heath. Lady Green, a former owner of the Hall, wrote a colourful history of the house, "The Old Hall at Heath", in which she includes a passage relating to the tomb of Lady Bolles:

At the foot is a singular little figure in alabaster, considered to be of a different and later date. Tradition has it that some doubt exists as to her really having, as tomb 'avers, "Departed this mortal life", a representation of her familiar spirit was added to prevent her walking the earth...Outside in the coach road and Hall field too, her apparition is to be met with, so the "familiar spirit" resemblance on her tomb seems inefficacious to stop her wanderings. The tomb at Ledsham Church which originally stood within the railings, close to the Communion Table, was lifted some twenty-yards to the North, outside the railing to give more space; when the masons were in the act of moving it, the church door opened unexpectedly, admitting a heavy gust of wind that blew the dust around the church for a second, then all fell silent again.

It is extraordinary that Mary's portent should come true, if only in part. For there were several members of the Whitham family, including old Whitam himself; yet up to now, only Lady Bolles has befallen the curse—leaving some room for the element of doubt as to whether or not Mary was hung for a sheep or a lamb. There is one point on which we can be reasonably sure: Mary is almost certain to have been subjected to the most horrendous ordeals in order to extract her confession, just as many others were to be in the not too distant future. Consequently, these poor, defenceless, illiterate creatures in the main willingly signed themselves to abominous statements. They openly declared their supposed allegiance to

*All that remains of the once beautiful period residence of Heath Old Hall,
near Wakefield—the home of Mary, Lady Bolles. She is alleged to still
haunt the ruins, mainly the steps at the front of the house and the coach
road that is now so badly overgrown. Mary, Lady Bolles' haunting occurs
each year on the 19th May.*

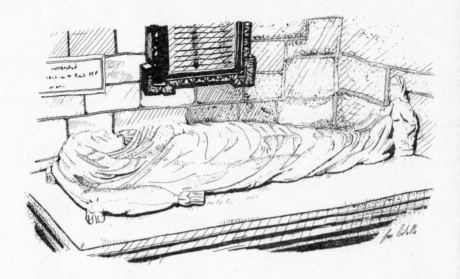

The tomb of Mary, Lady Bolles at Ledsham Church. On it has been placed an unusual alabaster figure, known locally as the 'witch figure'. The curious looking carving is of a later period than the tomb itself. It appears to have had little or no effect in holding down her restless, wandering spirit.

the devil in the vain hope of escaping further agonising pain and torment— only to find the noose or stake as their just reward.

Witchcraft is a very complex affair, with many diversities in its composition. Equally, there are parts of witchcraft we cannot label with an instantly recognisable name—like that part used by Mary Pennell, if indeed it was witchcraft at all. But with the Pendle witches, some three-years later, their use of the ancient craft is immediately identifiable—originating in the darker days of our primeval ancestors.

In 1612, two covens of witches, along with their leaders or high-priestesses, were discovered to be active in Pendle Forest, Lancashire, not far south of the Yorkshire boundary. The leaders were Elizabeth Southernes and Ann Whittle, alias, respectively, "old Demdike" and "old Chattox". They were arrested as a result of public unrest in the community, the main accusation being that they had employed the use of "magic" to murder certain of their neighbours. Old Demdike, of Malking Tower—a place described as most befitting for her profession—did not deny the charge as read. As to her methods, she stated that the easiest way to kill by witchcraft was to make "a picture of clay like unto the shape of the person" and to prick with a thorn or pin the parts where she desired her victim to feel the most pain. Should she wish to kill the victim outright in one fell swoop, this she achieved by burning the effigy altogether. Whereas, old Chattox, not wishing to openly confess herself in the same manner, said that old Demdike illustrated to her how she had done this to Richard Ashton—one of the witchcraft victims— but old

Demdike retaliated by accusing the other of the death of Robert Nutter.

Sir Edmund Bromley and Sir James Altham, assisted by one Mr Potts as their clerk, opened the assizes at Lancaster Castle on the 17th August, travelling directly from the assizes at York where they had recently concluded yet another witchcraft trial—that of Jennet Preston, who resided at Gisbourne-in-Craven. She was accused of bewitching to death Thomas Lister, of Westby—conveniently permitting me to relate the case of another notorious Yorkshire witch.

The victim, Thomas Lister, had thought well of this woman for a good many years, doing charitable favours for her from time to time. It was well known that she frequently visited his house, the Sowgill; but no clandestine assignations were ever thought to have evolved between the two. It was purely a relationship of merciful benefactor and grateful recipient, "nothing denied her she stood in need of" reads the record. Jennet Preston, however, was married at the time—her husband being "old Preston", who appears to have been content to let his wife beg for the both of them. Reginald Scott wrote of such women in his book **The Discoverie of Witchcraft** (an allegory that would also seem to fit Mary Pennell), first published in 1584:

These miserable wretches...go from house to house and from doore to doore for a pot of milke, yest, drinks, pottage, or some such releefe; without which they could hardlie live; neither obtaining for their service and paines, nor by their art, nor yet at the devil's hands (with whom they are said to make a perfect and visible bargaine) either beautie, monie, promotion, welth, worship, pleasure, honor, knowledge, learning, or anie other benefite whatsoever.

Jennet Preston's reputation as a witch was long established before this more recent accusation. At the previous Lent assizes at York, she faced similar charges for bringing about the death, by her disreputable means, of a child belonging to a Mr Dodge-sonnes (as Mr Potts recorded the name). As to the prosecutor of the case, here there seems to be some argument. On the one hand, it was said to have been Leonard Lister, the son of Thomas. On the other, according to certain evidence revealed at Lancaster some short time later (Jennet Preston's name being mentioned amongst the Pendle covens), it could well have been Thomas Lister himself. Whichever of the two, Jennet Preston believed that the prosecutor held a good deal of malice towards her, and thought he had it in mind to see her in gaol. But the verdict must have been to the contrary as she was subsequently acquitted of the charge.

Between the Lent and the next assizes at York, Thomas Lister mysteriously died, instantly bringing about a new charge against Jennet Preston. The clerk recorded: "Having cut off Thomas Lister Esq...she revenged herself upon his son, who in short time received great loss in his goods and cattel by her meanes." Her arrest, as later implied by the clerk, happened almost immediately after Lister's death. Whereupon, certain witnesses were called, who testified that the witch's victim, while laying on his death bed, had cried out that Jennet Preston was somewhere in the house.

As Thomas Lister's body was laid out, Jennet Preston was brought into the room and made to touch the corpse. As she did so, his body was said to have bled fresh blood in certain parts. This testimony was to be her undoing. On the 27th July, 1612, at York Castle, she was found guilty as charged. She was hanged shortly afterwards, dying impenetent and unconfessed. Her relatives and friends, apart from her husband that is, strongly professed her innocence. But old Preston was satisfied that justice had been seen to be done—his wife receiving no more than she rightfully deserved.

At Lancaster Castle, ten people in all were hanged for their nefarious antics in Pendle Forest. Eight others accused of witchcraft from Samlesbury, also tried at the same assizes, were more fortunate. They were found not guilty and released with a strong chiding from the prosecutor. As to old Demdike, she too was never to swing at the end of a rope, dying in prison during the trial. She surely would have had she lived long enough—she was the most prominent of all the accused.

Concerning the Pendle trials, however, in contrast to the later travesties of miscarried justice in the name of witch-persecution, there exist two very relevent factors that would imply the use of "true witchcraft". Firstly, old Demdike, described as "a very old woman about the age of four score years", and old Chattox, "a very old, withered, spent and decrepid creature of four score years", voluntarilly offered their confessions without the aid of torture and deprivation. One of the main reasons for this is thought to have been because of a long standing faction between the two women—each accusing the other by way of revenge. Even so, their willingness to admit to these gravest of charges with such a degree of unction must surely be unique in the annals of witch-trial history. But the second difference is of a far more convincing nature. Instead of the normal confessions expected from the accused—for example, the worshipping of the devil (which did eventually enter into their statements, though probably at the insistence of the inquisitor)—the women made claim to using "sympathetic magic" to do their dirty work by making clay effigies. And the thorough knowledge shown of these devices by old Demdike and old Chattox makes it more acceptable to believe that they truly were conjuring in the blackest of arts. In Philip W. Sergeant's book, **Witches and Warlocks**, he defines this part of witchcraft with clear elucidation:

One constituent of the whole is generally agreed to be the fertility cult, the notion of ability to influence the powers of nature to reproduce, whether it be men, beasts, or crops.

The fertility cult involves 'sympathetic magic', since there seemed apparently to that elusive person, primitive man, no other means of influencing nature. But sympathetic magic might be regarded as a separate constituent of witchcraft, being employed for other ends than the promoting of fertility. It may be desired by it to work not good but harm, notably injury to an enemy. From this we get the "blasting" power of the witches, exhibited either in procuring of death, in crippling, or in the stopping of generation—the antithesis of fertility-promotion.

This "magic" of old Demdike and old Chattox relied heavily upon the oldest of witchcraft principles—sheer, unadulterated fear. In evidence against old Chattox, it was heard that she made clay pictures of Christopher Nutter, Robert Nutter Jnr and his wife, Marie. Shortly afterwards Robert Nutter Jnr suddenly fell desperately ill and immediately suspected the cause. His brother, John, while offering his testimony to the court, said that as he was returning from Burnley to Pendle with his father and brother, he overheard Robert say: "Father, I am sure I am bewitched by Anne Chattox and Anne Redfearn. I pray you cause them to be laid in Lancaster Castle." His father admonished him harshly for harbouring such thoughts, telling his son not to be so foolish, but Robert was convinced that witchcraft was being used against him. He left the area and went to Wales, with the intention of soon returning. He was never to see Pendle again, dying in Cheshire on his homeward journey—less than six months after old Chattox had made his clay effigy. The relevant point is that Robert Nutter Jnr was fully aware of the witch's activities and fervently believed that she had the power to maim or kill him psychosomatically (a mutual relationship of mental phenomena and bodily conditions)—his mind and body together accepted his ill-fate as inevitable.

To the medieval mind, the concept of witchcraft was not very difficult to accept. And because of this ignorant comprehension, men like Matthew Hopkins—the "Witch Finder General"—were handed a golden opportunity in the guise of a witch-hunter. Lorenzo Padget, a local historian of the old West Riding in the late nineteenth century, stated that Hopkins was born at Altofts, near Castleford. But all other records show him to have been a kinsman of Ipswich, son of James Hopkins, a Puritan minister in the village of Wenham.

Being fairly well educated, Hopkins took up the law as his profession, first starting to practice in Ipswich itself—a venture that was not to prove entirely successful. Soon after, he moved to Manningtree, in Essex, where he was to see the real start of his true vocation. It was here, in 1645, that Matthew Hopkins realised just how bounteous this contemptible work as a freelance witch-hunter could be—charging a not too modest fee for every conviction he obtained by fair means or foul. In deadly earnest, his campaign of agony and death began. At Chelmsford market place alone, in a single afternoon, he sent no less than nineteen women to the gallows. Similarly, he arrived at Huntingdon in hot pursuit of new quarry. But here, indifferent to his expectations, for the first time he was to face heavy criticism from a local clergyman—John Gaule, vicar of Great Haughton. The Rev. Gaule struck out verbally at the Witch Finder, accusing him of being a hypocrit and an agitator. Also, in his pamphlet, "Select Cases of Conscience Touching Witches and Witchcraft", he made reference to Hopkins' easy targets: "Every old woman with a wrinkled face, a furrowed brow, a hairy lip, a gibber tooth, a squint eye, a squeaking voice, or a scolding tongue..." Ordinary, harmless old women, yet they would readily bring condemnation from the self-professed devil's denouncer, not to mention a speedy profit.

Stowmarket was another area to which Hopkins made himself and his deplorable talents available, asking a token of twenty-shillings from every town he rid of its witches. After torturing and executing in excess of sixty women, he earned in the region of £28 from this single enterprise. Old John Lowes, the eighty-year old reading parson of Brandeston, was amongst his Suffolk victims. He was sentenced to death, but not before being "swum"—for causing a ship to sink at sea. It must have been the Flying Dutchman, for although exhaustive inquiries were made, no such vessel could be traced.

The "swimming" of witches was a common practice of Hopkins and his henchmen. They would tie the accused's thumbs and big toes together with rope before throwing them into a pond or deep stream. If they sank, providence was with them—but if they floated, it was certain death. King James I himself approved of this barbaric test, and recorded as much in his book **Demonologie**: "The water shall refuse to receive them in her bosum that have shaken off them the Sacred Water of Baptisme, and wilfullie refused the benefite thereof".

37

The "walking" and "pricking" of witches were even more distasteful measures adopted by the persecutors. The "walking" method was done mainly to deprive the accused of rest. Incessantly, for up to two or three days and nights, they would be paced to and fro, supported by two paid watchers. Ultimately, they would become so fatigued both mentally and physically that they would willingly confess to any number of crimes—out of their sheer desperation for rest.

By far, Hopkins would best be remembered as a searcher of the devil's mark. In the case of a male prisoner the task he would undertake himself, whereas Goody Phillips was his regular female searcher. Carefully the accused's body was scrutinised for spots, blemishes, birth-marks, even moles —all considered by Hopkins to be unnatural "papps or teats" upon which the devil was supposed to feed. If any were found, and they invariably were, these they would prick with a bradawl-like instrument, maybe up to five or six times in all, causing the pain to reach an insurmountable level. At this point the accused would appear not to feel any more pricking—Hopkins then declaring them a witch and obtaining his fee.

There are many accounts of his final retreat from this bloody business. One has it that he too was hanged for a witch. But the parish register of Mistley-cum-Manningtree shows that he was buried on the 12th August, 1647, after dying peacefully in his own bed. Hutchinson's **Historical Essay on Witchcraft** suggests that Matthew Hopkins "went on searching and swimming the poor creatures until some gentleman, out of indignation at the barbarity, took him and tied his own thumbs and toes, as he used to tye others, and when he was put into the water he himself swam as well as they did. This cleared the country of him, and it was a great deal of pity that they did not think of the experiment before." But this story was more probably brought about by wishful thinkers.

Retrospectively, is it right that all the blame be pinned on Hopkins and his kind? After all, the reason for him acquiring such acclaim was a direct result of public demand. Nevertheless, his motto: "Thou shalt not suffer a witch to live", must surely have struck terror into the hearts of young and old alike— for no one was safe when the Witch Finder General was abroad in the district.

Strikingly, today some of us can still accept the medieval comprehension of witchcraft. There is an active coven of witches in Leeds at this very moment in time. But these are a far cry from the witches of old. For some, it has become a pitiful excuse for sexual titillation; for others, it may be the stirrings of ancient, primeval instincts—witchcraft undoubtedly seeing its origins with primitive man. Only with the assistance of an inborn fear of the unnatural, combined with superstition, has it been nurtured over the passing generations. In a modern society, thankfully, "true witchcraft" cannot effectively work, the reason being that we dismiss "magic" as a fantasy subject better left in children's fairytales. Progress has lifted the blinkers of ignorance, removing all traces of the malevolent aspect of witchcraft, allowing it to disappear into obscurity—where it rightfully belongs.

5: Spiritualism and the Rescue Medium

AT A RURAL farmhouse belonging to the Fox family, in Hydesville, New York, sometime in the month of March 1848 an unnatural disturbance was to cause the birth of perhaps the most unusual and controversial religion ever to be conceived—Spiritualism. It began with strange, loud, tapping sounds, not unlike the noisy trademark of the poltergeist—which kept the family awake at all hours of the night. But choose how much they searched for a culprit, the source was never to be detected. Then, suddenly, late one evening, the break-through finally came. Kate, aged twelve, and the youngest of the Fox sisters, began clicking her fingers for no apparent reason, as children are want to do. To the family's amazement, the tapping sounds began to imitate her. It also happened, purely by chance, that an inquisitive neighbour had called to visit, under some inane pretence, although the truth was more likely to have been as a result of local gossip. But this woman's presence turned out to be an invaluable asset, for she hit upon the idea of asking it, whatever it was, questions via a simple code system—one tap for "yes", and two taps for "No". The technique seemed to work, but only questions involving numbers could be answered with any degree of accuracy. For example, it tapped out individually the ages of all those present. At this point the inquisitive neighbour turned out to be even more resourceful by coming up with an extension of her original idea. This was to make up an alphabetical code, which would then enable them to ask more detailed questions.

Accordingly, through this latter method the phantom tapper identified itself as the departed spirit of a pedlar named Charles B. Rosmar, who had been murdered in the house some five years previously. Excitedly, they asked for more information. The murder had taken place in the east bedroom, Rosma being killed by having his throat cut and then buried in the cellar. As a result of the spirit's claims the police were called in to investigate, but they failed to find the remains of the missing pedlar—and the enquiry ended abruptly. (In 1904, a wall collapsed in the cellar of the farmhouse to reveal a male skeleton, and lying by its side a pedlar's box.)

Some days later the situation altered into a more common form of haunting with eerie sounds of a struggle and a body being dragged across a bedroom floor. In the meantime, the tapping noises followed the Fox sisters around from house to house. The local inhabitants were becoming increasingly agitated at this odd behaviour. Consequently it was decided, by one of the various committees formed to try and catch the girls out, to completely separate the sisters. But this only antagonised the problem. For when Kate and Margaret Fox were split up and put into separate dwellings, the tapping noises broke out in both houses.

Calvin Brown, a man who lived in the same house as Leah Fox, the eldest sister, was rather hostile towards her. The spirit somehow detected this and began to throw things at him—uncannily, without doing him any actual injury. Mrs Fox had to get used to the nuisance of having her lace-cap snatched off by invisible hands, or the comb in her hair pulled out. The rest of the family had to endure the painful experience of having pins stuck into them whenever they knelt to say prayers.

As time went by, the tapping noises became unbearable. One report has it that they could be heard more than a mile away from the house. Growing desperate for a solution, they again decided to try and communicate with the spirit by means of the alphabetical code. But this time the message they received was far more daunting. It said: "Dear Friends, you must proclaim this truth to the world. This is the dawning of a new era."

From those very words the inaugural Spiritualist Meeting was held on the 14th November, 1849. Six months later the news of the new religion slowly permeated throughout America, eventually finding its way across the Atlantic to Europe. Its first mediums were all three of the Fox sisters. Since this time the spirit's request has been carried out to the letter—for the Spiritualist Church has grown into a vast organisation recognised the world over.

Here in England, however, this new religion was to undergo a serious setback, for its emergence coincided with the founding of the Society for Psychical Research (S.P.R.), an august body intent upon investigating every element of the unnatural with a view to establishing the existence of psychic phenomena. It furnished corroborative proof to show that many of the so-called "mediums" often employed fraudulent tricks when conducting seances, a situation which made it increasingly difficult for the few genuine mediums to work unfettered and unimpeded.

In contrast to their Victorian and Edwardian counterparts, present day mediums gladly offer themselves to be tested at scientific institutes under laboratory controlled conditions. Just as with the early pioneers of the S.P.R., the modern Spiritualist Church and its members wish only to determine whether or not their often amazing talents are indeed of a true psychic nature. These mediums are as diverse as their religion; not all of them adopt the same methods but all of them endeavour for the same results—all, that is, with the exception of the "Rescue Medium". This branch of Spiritualism offers a precise and exact service—far removed from the Noel Coward 1920s image of a batty, middle-aged Madam Arcarty, seated in a dingy, cluttered parlour, constantly wailing: "Is there anyone there?" For this type of medium would be better described as a "layer of ghosts".

In 1980, by a curious turn of fate, I was introduced to such a medium, Mr Harold Turford, of Old Sharlston, near Wakefield, by my own brother—the reason for emphasising "my own brother" being that he is a born sceptic. But even he seems to have been impressed by Mr Turford's reasoning. I now have to mention Mr Turford's name in a past tense, for in 1981 he died suddenly while visiting his son in Germany. Thankfully, he told me how he

40

had first become a Spiritualist and subsequent "rescue medium" a good while prior to this sad event. His story is worthy of the telling, not out of sympathy but because he truly was a most remarkable individual.

His story begins during the conflict with the Japanese in the steamy, tropical jungles of Burma and India when he was still only tender in years and yet already seasoned in the arena of active service. One of his fondest recollections of this hostile period was the memory of a young seepoy he had met—an Indian of the highest cast, a Brahman, by the name of Rham Kishor. Their meeting, as will later be revealed, was a pre-ordained affair. The two were of a similar age but each segregated by different worlds with so very different values. Harold Turford wasn't to realise it at the time, but he was very fortunate in that he saw India through the eyes of Rham Kishor. It was an India full of mysticism and the ancient ways of the East—market places teaming with life, snake charmers and the miracle working Fakirs. Some of these delights can still be seen in the majority of Indian cities and townships—and even some of the smaller villages. But the greatest illusion of the street magicians, the Indian rope trick, was solved many years ago by Kipling. The Fakirs would cunningly use the power of mass-hypnosis, fooling their audience into believing whatever they were told to believe. Anyone who didn't understand the language was to be disappointed, for he would see nothing of the fantastic extravaganza.

One afternoon Rham Kishor took Harold on a trip to a settlement out in the wilds. It was a torridly hot day, with brilliant sunshine streaming through verdant trees. A profusion of gayly coloured birds flittered above their heads as they walked towards a very old Guru seated in the shade. He was clad in a white sarong, and looked the very image of India itself. A faint breeze swirled the dust across the parched ground as Rham Kishor led Harold to the feet of the sage. Their greeting was of the classic Hindu style, rigid with hands clasped as if in prayer, curtailed by a gentle bowing action. The old man reciprocated by slowly nodding his head, though he never lifted his eyes from his constant gaze at the floor. The two young men sat down beside him. It was peaceful here, and a vast contrast to the hellish noises of war, so much so that they lingered for a while and savoured the simplicity of the setting.

In all this time the ancient never spoke. But just as they were about to get up to leave the old man began to scrawl a message with his finger in a pile of yellow sand. For Harold's benefit, Rham Kishor translated the message which read: "One who will see beyond the grave." Neither of them understood what this implied, for Harold's strange ability had not yet come to light.

Some weeks later, Harold and a comrade were on a jungle patrol when they found themselves in a very tight spot. To their backs were the Japanese; before them, a sprawling river with strong and very dangerous currents. And as if the situation wasn't desperate enough, Harold had been wounded in the thigh. What's more, his comrade, Paddy Reap, couldn't swim a stroke. As dusk fell the two men had little alternative but to dig themselves in. Several yards from them, the bank of the river raised itself to form a kind of hillock. Harold was concentrating on this, when a strange apparition appeared before him in a veil of swirling mist. It was the spirit of his grandfather Wood, only recognisable from old family photographs, for Harold and the old man had never actually met. He emigrated to Canada when his grandson was little more than a babe-in-arms—dying there some years later. The spirit was pointing a very long, thin, waxen finger in the direction of the far shore of the river. That would be their only salvation. In fact, the spirit said as much in a soft, whispering voice.

There was no moon that night as they took to the water. Under one arm nestled Paddy Reap, under the other a piece of wood for a float. But with Harold now was something he had never experienced before, a strong surge of power which felt to be driving him on. His fortitude revitalised and much strengthened, a new found courage was running wildly through his veins which enabled him to carry out this enormous feat of human endurance. The two men were found the following morning, thankfully, by a British patrol; they were unconscious and lifeless, but providence was with them— they had survived the rigorous crossing.

Shortly after a spell in hospital, Harold was sent back into active service, this time to join the West Yorks, a composite battalion. The Japanese were still swarming the country and jungle warfare was evidently taking its toll. Within a few short months, on a second occasion Harold was to feel the magnitude of this awesome power surge through his body and save his life yet again. They were on the banks of the Cheduin, a dried up river basin, when through the stillness a voice came to him saying: "Darky, don't go down the chong, don't go down the chong." (Darky being his nickname in the forces—and chong meaning the river basin.) When the Japanese struck there was a great deal of confusion. Men were running in all directions. But the fates were with Harold; he didn't go down the chong, as most of the others did—instead he escaped through dense jungle. His friend, Rham Kishor, had not been so fortunate; he was killed in the affray of the attack.

Not long after this, Harold returned to England. He didn't come home empty handed, for within him now remained this new enlightenment. Spiritualism seemed to offer the most obvious conclusion. Understandably, he wanted to know specifically why the two visitations had come to him. Why had he, above all others, been singled out? Perhaps, through the Spiritualist Church these questions might be answered.

At the very first meeting he attended—orchestrated by a Mr William Ogden, with C.I. Quastel the speaker and the chairperson being J.W. Dawson—the medium told Harold that his grandfather was standing directly behind him. To begin with he was a trifle sceptical, and tried to think of a way to make sure the medium wasn't faking. In response, he asked if it was possible for him to be supplied with the full name of the spirit. Without hesitation, the medium replied: "Lewis Edward Wood", followed by his grandfather's old address in England—even adding the information that this man had been one of the first active unionists at Frickley Colliery. The medium went on to mention the importance of the last meeting between the two. But Harold stressed that he had no recollection of any such meeting—he being a tiny baby at the time of his grandfather's departure for Canada. Again, the medium did not faulter, and went on to say that he could see a young man with blood on his thigh. This young man had definitely been a soldier in the Far Eastern theatre of war. There was also a wide river, and an overpowering urge to swim to safety.

At this point everything dropped into perspective. Harold went cold from head to foot, as in his mind he recalled that terrible night. He **had** seen his grandfather, standing on the banks of the river—their last meeting which turned out to be very important indeed.

The war well and truly over, it was time to settle down in a job. This took the form of a shot-firer; oddly enough at the same colliery his grandfather had worked in all those years ago—Frickley, South Elmsall. To Harold's displeasure, more often than not he had to work the day or early shift and be up at four in the morning. Even though his work would be finished by one in the afternoon, he was always too tired to appreciate the rest of the day. It wasn't surprising then that he took to having an afternoon nap on the bed. And it was during his habitual afternoon repose when he got his first real glimpse of his spirit guide—a mentor, chosen by a much higher authority for all psychics.

Laying on his back, looking up at the ceiling, the light fading as it was becoming dusk, he suddenly became aware of a presence in the room. Not a physical presence, but one of another dimension. The atmosphere had turned clammy and icy-cold. At first, this presence did not show itself. Overcome with a compelling sensation of fear, he broke into a struggling panic, as he felt the presence come closer and closer to the bed. A strange force-like pressure pinned him down flat to the mattress, making it impossible for him to move. He tried to call out: "Mother! Mother!" but no sound would issue from his lips. Then he saw it, the contorted face of Rham Kishor, pushing ever so close to his. But with the vision came a new euphoria. A soothing voice, a voice he recognised instantly, whispered: "My brother". Simultaneously all his fears diminished and in their place was a soothing calm. Afterwards Harold felt drained yet filled with a curious contentment.

The National Union of Spiritualism, of which he later became an important member, organises classes for the development of mediumistic qualities. Harold readily accepted the opportunity and persevered with his tuition for two years or more. But along the way he grew disillusioned with the idea. For some unknown reason he left the church, and even his home and job—and went to live and work in Scotland. This disillusionment, however, was not to be of a very permanent nature, for he soon found himself attending a meeting at the Rosyth Spiritualist Church.

The service was supposed to commence at seven sharp, only there was an unforeseen problem. The lady who was to conduct the proceedings had forgotten to make appropriate arrangements for her transport home. The dilemma was that her last bus left early and a taxi was out of the question. Faced, then, with the prospect of a long and lonely walk home in the dark, she had no alternative but to take the bus. Irrespective of the consequences, the congregation would have to get on as best they could without her, leaving two possibilities open to them—either they all went home, in which case the evening had been wasted, or they found someone else to take the meeting.

After an interminable period of debate, it was accidentally discovered that Harold had done some schooling in mediumship—and he was cordially invited to take the floor. Initially his refusal, which was only to be understood, was adamant. He had never addressed a public meeting before,

43

and was reluctant to even consider the idea at such short notice. Yet after being subjected to a good deal of gentle persuasion, and just as much friendly encouragement, he finally gave way to their demands. After all, there was one consolation, he could be rest assured that if he made a bad job of it this time he would never be asked again.

Clambering to his feet, weak-kneed and trembling, he made his way to the front of the hall. As he walked that vital energy he first felt out in India began to pulsate within him. With each step it grew stronger, more vibrant, until he reached the platform itself where his confidence came flooding back. And with the aid of Rham Kishor, his spirit guide, the meeting proved to be a success. This indescribable force had twice saved his life, terrified him by its very existence, and now permitted him to do things he never dreamt himself capable of doing. From that evening in the small church at Rosyth, his talents were to develop more acutely. His interest in Spiritualism no longer subdued, his previous misgivings disappeared overnight, leaving him convinced that he had chosen the right direction.

Towards the end of the 1960s, Harold Turford, now living back in Yorkshire, was invited to London by a group of eminent Spiritualist mediums. They had a rather strange request to make of him. A Russian astronaut had had a fatal accident in outerspace, trapping his spirit for all eternity in the great black void. They wanted Harold, along with his wealth of experience, to assist them in forming a psychic link—a subconscious step ladder by which the wayward spirit could return home. As to whether the experiment worked—he never said.

At the time of making his acquaintance, in what was probably the last incident he was called on to deal with, Harold had recently been asked to lay a spirit to rest which was causing a nuisance at a terraced house in a small, local mining village. A young couple, along with their recently-born baby, lived in the house. And it was because of the child, in a roundabout way, that the ghostly visitor came calling.

In the early evening, the mother would put her baby to bed in the bedroom directly above the living room. But as the night progressed, she would hear hollow sounding footsteps overhead, walking from the direction of the bedroom door and halting in the vicinity of the child's cot. To begin with, the ghostly footsteps were only heard by the mother. One night in particular, when her husband was out at work, the footsteps came with the strongest audible clarity. Being anxious for the safety of the child, she went to investigate. As she pushed open the bedroom door, the night light cast an eerie glow on the walls and ceiling. Her eyes immediately focused on the cot in the corner of the room. What she saw was only vague, shadow-like, but recognisable. Leaning over the rail of the cot, looking closely at the sleeping child, was the figure of an old woman.

Later that evening, when her husband returned home, she told him of what she had seen. At first, with an air of rationality, he informed his wife of the fact that ghosts do not exist—they are figments of the imagination. He was soon to change his tune, for he personally witnessed the appearance of the old woman not long afterwards. Turning to a neighbour for advice, who happened to be a friend of Mr Turford's, he suggested that they contact Harold as soon as possible—no doubt, he would know what to do for the best.

Almost a week later, in the early evening, Harold arrived, accompanied by the informative neighbour. The four of them went on up to the bedroom, where Harold began to investigate. The baby was already fast asleep in the cot, and the night light was gently burning on a small chest of drawers. It was necessary for him to first check-out the possibilities of natural causes for the apparition, such as a light reflecting on a window. Perhaps the footsteps were nothing more than the floorboards creaking as the house settled down for the night—but he found no such evidence.

All they could do was wait. The group returned to the living room, where cups of tea were cordially handed round. Their wait, however, was to be shorter than anticipated—for it wasn't long before they all heard the footsteps overhead. A slight but orderly rush broke out for the stairs, Harold in the lead. The bedroom door had been left ajar. He entered the room first while the neighbour took up a sentinel-like position by the door jamb. As the neighbour saw the figure, his face became quite ashen as he had known the old woman for many years when she had been alive. Harold approached the apparition and asked her why she was here. In the faintest voice, she replied that she merely wanted to look at the baby. Reassuringly, he explained that she could easily do this without showing herself—her appearance was causing the child's parents a considerable amount of unnecessary anxiety. The old woman was a very understanding soul. With no further ado, she slowly faded to nothing. Invisible, she was welcome to visit the child whenever she pleased. Successively, the footsteps had also been quietened—never to be heard again.

During a later conversation with the nerve-shaken neighbour, Harold discovered the identity of the old woman. Apparently, she had lived in that same house all her married life, given birth to and raised her own children there, and finally, when her life was over, had died there.

According to Harold Turford, he performed a normal, everyday function. His reasoning was based around a simplistic ideology. When a body dies, the soul or spirit it housed can and often does lose its way. Their only resolve is to return to familiar surroundings—to the places they most frequented during their mortal existence. All Harold Turford did, or any other rescue medium for that matter, was to put them back on the right road. No mention of blood-thirsty murders, or disquieting suicides. It is easy to lose one's way, we do it often enough throughout life—why not in death?

Although many of Harold Turford's experiences have been found coercive —with witnesses offering substantiated evidence—I feel it right to point out that, hypothetically, other mediums of the more ordinary variety whose talents lay in the conducting of seances can be defined, to some extent, in a psychological context.

In 1922 Freud, the father of psychoanalysis,—inclinated that telepathy used to be an active part of our mental constitution. He deduced this from observing relationships between analysts and patients, where, in many cases, the two had built up a sort of telepathic rappore. He also confirmed his growing interest for this train of thought when writing a letter to Ernest Jones, a colleague and author of Freud's biography, who happened to be a hardent sceptic. Freud made the following comments after looking into the experiments of Gilbert Murray on thought transferrence:

45

> I confess that the impression made by these reports was so strong that I am ready to give up my opposition to the existence of thought-transference...I should even be prepared to lend the support of psychoanalysis to the matter of telepathy.

Unfortunately, Jones was not willing to succeed to these claims, describing them as "dangerous" and detrimental to psychoanalysis. Through him, Freud was prevented from reading an essay on the subject, "Psychoanalysis and Telepathy", at the International Psychoanalytical Congress in 1922. This was not published until after Freud's death in 1941.

But consider for a moment the possibility that mediums also use a "telepathic link" between themselves and those in attendance at a seance. Does the medium receive messages from the dead—or the subconsciousness of those in attendance? A very relevant example of this theory can be found in Rosalind Heywood's book **The Sixth Sense**, where she includes a summary of an article by an Italian psychoanalyst, Emilio Servadio, from which this passage is taken:

> Freud suggested that telepathy may be the original archaic method by which individuals understood each other, but that it has been pushed into the background by methods of communication via the senses, which are more efficient. The older methods may still manifest themselves under certain conditions. He also came to think that some people might become aware by telepathy of the conscious or unconscious phantasies of others and express these in a distorted fashion. The distortion might take the form of displacing a past event into the future or of transferring one person's experiences to someone else...

Much of this passage could be interpreted as describing "mediumistic qualities"—whereby, the medium, being "aware by telepathy of the conscious or unconscious phantasies of others...", then endeavours to reveal "a past event into the future...transferring one person's experiences to someone else..." It is almost an exact replica of what can be expected at a seance.

This may not have a plausible ring of truth to some; but to others, whose preferment lies with a scientific explanation, then hopefully this hypothesis may inspire a little food for thought.

6: A Pot-Pourri of Hermits, Wise Old Women, Wizards and Superstitions

THE SOCIAL structure of the middle-ages altered considerably after the traumatic events of the dissolution. Gone were the over-prosperous abbots, the bench of bishops and the merry fat friars. But amongst these theocratic refugees, there was another, though slightly less unsung casualty of this deadly battle between Church and Throne; one who, unlike his monastic contemporaries, was never destined fully to re-emerge—the hermit. This now extinct breed, however, appear to have been blessed with much more than saintly piety—healing powers, the gift of prophecy, and, if the story of the "Penny Hedge" at Whitby is to be taken into account, it would also seem that their wrath was something never to be roused.

Long, long ago, so the story has it, there lived in the beautiful woodland of Eskdale, a monk from the abbey at Whitby who had chosen to live the life of a solitary. There, within his tiny chapel surrounded by the splendours of nature, he contented himself with the simple virtues of prayer. Until, one misty October morning, there came upon the scene three sporting gentlemen—William de Bruce, Ralph de Piercie, and another who remains anonymous—along with their hounds to hunt a ferocious, giant boar whose reputation had reached the furthermost parts of the county. This mighty beast of fearsome distinction was also an inhabitant of the great forest at Eskdale, the area then belonging to St. Hilda's monastery at Whitby.

Good fortune must have been with the huntsmen that day for the beast was soon routed, and a lengthy and frantic chase ensued. At one point, the fleeing, raged animal came so close that the huntsmen were able to inflict deep, penetrating wounds. However, the beast was worthy of some praise, it managing to elude its captors for a good long while—the chase ending rather abruptly when the helpless boar rushed into the hermit's chapel. Startled, but seeing the poor animal's terrible plight, the hermit slammed the door on the fast approaching pack. At his feet, the boar spilled its lifeblood while, outside, the baying hounds sang a deathly chorus.

When the huntsmen arrived at the chapel the beast was dead, which caused them to grow to such anger for they had not been privileged to witness "the kill". Cursing the hermit for his meddling interference, in an uncontrolled outburst of temper the three men set about him with their swords and brutally attacked the defenceless sage. Leaving him for dead, his assailants, knowing full well the extent of their heartless crime, rode forth with all speed to Scarborough—there to beg for sanctuary. But unknown to them, the abbot of Whitby was a loyal and trusted friend of the king. And because of this, royal consent was instantly granted to apprehend the huntsmen, in the hope that they suffered the full penalty of the law—death for death.

The three men would surely have hanged but for one intervention, a saving grace. Before the hermit died he forgave his merciless attackers, but they were not to get away too lightly. As every sinner, they must do penance for their wrongful actions, the hermit himself describing their atonement:

Once a year upon Ascension Eve they, and their successors, shall enter this wood at sunrise, receive from an officer at the Abbey ten stakes, ten stout stowers and ten yedders apiece (props and pliant branches for intertwining) cut with a penny knife. These they must carry on their backs; and at low water they shall each build a hedge, each stake a yard from the other, and they shall so yedder them with yedders and so stake on each side with stout stowers that they stand three tides without being washed away. This they, and their successors, shall do in memory of their crime; and the better to call this deed to remembrance one shall sound a horn, and another cry, "Out on you, out on you, out on you!" And if they, or their successors, fail thus to build a hedge that shall withstand three tides, the lands they now hold shall be forfeit to the Abbey at Whitby.

Curiously, the hermit's almost curse-like words have been stringently obeyed for more than nine-hundred years. The "Penny Hedge" is still built on the eve of Ascension Day by Arthur Hutton on behalf of his cousin, George Hutton—the present owner of the land which would still become forfeit to the abbey should the custom not be carried out.

As to some hermits being the beholders of prophetic powers, this was to be the undoing of one thirteenth-century Yorkshire recluse. While Richard was busying himself in the Holy Land, bringing the marauding infidel to heel, John, his brother and self-instated king of England, was visited by a strange old man—Peter, the hermit of Pontefract. This old man had had a vision of great importance to the king. It announced a sharp curtailment to Johns presumptive reign. So disturbed was he by the contents of the vision, which came to him in the form of a dream, that he felt duty-bound to walk all the way from Pontefract to London, where he could personally deliver his prophecy at first hand.

For John's amusement, the foot-sore prophet was ushered in and permitted to speak of his vision. But when John heard the full gist of the vision, to which the old man had gone to such pains to deliver, his attitude changed to heated anger. For this affrontery, the hermit was dragged from the court, pitilessly tortured and subsequently executed. His head was severed from his body and stuck on a pikestaff by the gates of London, there to remain as a sore reminder to other would-be prophets bearing ill-tidings for the king. Rough justice indeed for the poor anchorite, particularly when his prediction of John's downfall was most accurate—John being deposed soon after.

Peter was by no means the first hermit of Pontefract—that honour lies with Roger de Laythorp. His hermitage, although inaccessible to the general public, remains intact beneath the old dispensary of Pontefract General Infirmary. A series of three caves, laboriously hand-hewn out of the solid rock: it is mysterious, dark, eerie and unusually beautiful. The first chamber is composed like an anteroom, with two carved stone benches, one on either side of the doorway—a place for the hermit's patrons to await an audience. Leading from here, and classed as the second cave, is a stone spiral staircase descending some fifty-feet to the third chamber. In this somewhat confined space the hermit lived. A small altar stands by the wall, where mass was said daily by one of the monks from the nearby Franciscan priory of St. Richard. The only other evidence of the hermit's lifestyle is a stone trough in the corner, a receptacle built around the head of an underground freshwater spring. The atmosphere is as strange now as it must have appeared to weary medieval travellers who wished to ask the hermit to pray for their safe conduct. By the doorway to the lowest cave, inscribed in the rock, there reposes a skeleton, the "Morte-Memorium"—remember death, it comes for all, irrespective of wealth, rank or position.

The remarkable thing about this hermitage is that many weird apparitions have been seen to manifest in its vicinity. Colin Wilson, that doyen of the paranormal, recently had occasion to visit the area to investigate an outbreak of poltergeist activity, the case of "The Black Monk of Pontefract", the story of which is included in his book, **Poltergeist**. At the end of a moderately lengthy chapter about the incident, he draws the following conclusion:

I am suggesting, then, that the solution to the mystery of the Black Monk of Pontefract may lie in the ground itself. It is "haunted" ground, land that retains impressions for a long time. Only a few days before I arrived in Pontefract, a nursing sister at the Pontefract General Infirmary...came into the television room. There were two other members of staff there, and she noticed, as she sat down, that there was also a man in a dressing gown. Patients were not allowed in that room, and after a moment she turned her head to look at the man. He was no longer there—yet he could not have left the room without walking past her; he had been sitting in the corner. This, then, is my own theory about the Black Monk case. The ground itself contains some peculiar force that favours "manifestations".

I wonder if Roger de Laythorp also realised that this "peculiar force" was present on the site—and was thus encouraged to build his hermitage here in the first place. My reason for putting this question stems from the unusual air of mysticism that was always associated with the hermit. Although not full-blooded occultists in the literal sense, they were very esoteric in their practices. Likewise, many of them did possess certain skills that were not altogether the norm—but I'm not too sure that dowsing for Ley Lines was one of them. The dowser believes that under the earth's surface and invisible to the naked eye, there exists a series of lines—channels of powerful energy which are considered to be capable of influencing psychic-phenomena. The theory has it that these lines are supposed to connect up with all the prehistoric sites, such as Stone Henge and Avebury, forming a huge network covering the length and breadth of the country—a neolithic national grid. But as to how this power was tapped and to what purpose it served will remain a secret of the ancient priests. There is no mention, however, of Roger de Laythorp being anything other than a religious recluse. Nevertheless, if the reports of the night staff are anything to go by, the Infirmary at Pontefract must have more ghosts per square yard than any other building in the country.

Unlike that rara-avis the Phoenix, the hermit did not resurface from the ashes, whereas wise old women were to be a common feature in Yorkshire right up until as recently as the nineteenth century. These were women to whom the country folk turned for charms when the cream in the churn refused to become butter, or for a cure for toothache, or if a beast suddenly fell ill for no apparent reason. One such old woman, hailing from Thorpe Audlin, had a widespread reputation for making love potions. But the most outlandish of them all has to be, without doubt, the old woman of

Darrington.

Even as late as the 1870s, country people strenuously believed that it was possible for fearsome creatures to dwell within one's interior organs. These were thought to have their origins in water drunk from a running stream or wayside rivulet. Anyone who suddenly developed an enormous appetite as a regular thing was believed to harbour one. This old woman of Darrington was particularly noted for finding an effective cure for this odd malady, her remedy being to starve the patient, along with the unwelcome parasite, until both were ravenously hungry. Then she would cook an appealing dish under the sufferer's nose, so that the Eft, as these creatures were called, would leap forth out of his mouth. Fried onions mixed with sage and thyme was her most often used recipe.

J.S. Fletcher, a previously mentioned local historian, who happened to live in the same village before he moved on to better things, personally interviewed the old woman I refer to for his book **Memories of a Spectator** at the turn of the century:

There was an old woman living near the Methodist Chapel at Darrington about 1870 who had two Efts, stuffed and varnished, hanging among papers and dried herbs over her chimneypiece, which she asserted she had drawn from sufferers... It was this same old woman...who, being then, well over a hundred years old, told me her personal narrative respecting the doings of a certain man who used to live in the woods at Stapleton and was reported to be a wizard. She said that at times he used to wear strange robes with curious devices painted on them; that he had a cat in which a certain spirit dwelt; that a dead man's hand, cured, hung over his mantlepiece (thought to be the same hand as mentioned in the first chapter, "The Hand of Glory"), and that he could do all manner of strange things after reading out of his books, of which he had a great many, more, she said, than the parson had...This last of the wise men used to be fee'd by the farmers about Darrington Leys to charm the crops; he also had the power of raising evil spirits, and my old woman asserted that she once saw him at midnight in his own garden in company with a tall person in black garments, who vanished in a flash of lightning when she, having made the sign of the cross, repeated the Lord's prayer backwards.

She sounds to have been a very colourful character. But without such women, it must be said that many important drugs and medicines would have been a lot longer in their discovery. An example is digitalis, made from the leaves of the purple Foxglove—for many centuries, country women prepared infusions of these leaves for the treatment of dropsy. Its more common use is to slow down and strengthen the heart beat in the treatment of cardiac diseases. Or, there is Bella Donna, a sleeping draft and muscle relaxant made from the Deadly Nightshade, which contains the alkaloids atropine and hyoscyamine. The name Bella Donna (Beautiful Lady) was given to it because Italian ladies used the drug to enlarge their pupils as an aid to beauty. According to the belief of the herbalist, almost every variety of plant and herb contained some healing quality. But without the knowledge of "old wives" passed on from one generation to another, these often life-giving, seemingly miraculous properties would have remained undiscovered until who knows when.

On a more macabre note, in the seventeenth century a moss which was found to grow on old skulls was used to treat an assortment of nervous disorders. Although a deviation from the main theme, but pertinent to skulls, this brings to mind the story of Anne Griffith at Burton Agnes Hall near Bridlington.

Anne Griffith was violently struck down by a band of thieves after she caught them plundering the house. Her wounds were mortal, but before she died she made her family promise that they would remove her head from her body and keep it within the confines of the hall. Understandably, her family assumed that her odd request was the ramblings of delirium, but their assumption could not have been further from the truth. Shortly after her death, Anne's ghost appeared, in tune to much door slamming and doleful moaning, continuing to show her displeasure towards the family for them not adhering to her wishes. Unable to withstand her ghostly antics, they decided to re-open the grave and bring her skull inside the house, whereupon the hauntings ceased. They would no doubt have continued in that vein had it not been for a thoughtless servant, who, inadvertently, cast the skull out into the garden. Spontaneously, the hauntings recommenced. The family then came up with a better idea whereby the skull was returned to the house and bricked into a wall—where it still remains. Anne Griffith's spirit is peacefully at rest for most of the time, but she occasionally re-appears— perhaps checking to make sure the skull has not been removed.

Equally interesting was the skull of Bowland Hall, which belonged to a victim of Henry VIII's tragic onslaught in Yorkshire, caused by the failing of the insurrection so aptly titled "the Pilgrimage of Grace". When the skull was removed from the hall, several deaths, among other unnatural disturbances, occurred in the family—ceasing only when the skull had been returned.

How the idea of keeping skulls inside first materialised has never been fully determined, and it is doubtful if it ever will be. But according to speculation, it could have originated from one of two sources; either it had some significant connection with the primitive ritual of "foundation sacrifice", or, under a more gruesome supposition, it was a reminder of our savage past and the gory custom of "head-hunting" as practised by the Celts.

Returning to the subject at hand, I can find no other reference alluding to the wizard of Darrington Leys—but his existence is highly likely. Rural folk seem to have been more affected by these people than, say, town or city dwellers. This could have been brought about by their living much closer to nature and the natural processes their daily lives so greatly depended upon. Farmers in particular were a superstitious lot, and a wizard on the payroll would have been an opportunity too good to miss—the wizard being thought to have had control over weather conditions.

Even today, it is no uncommon sight to see the ash tree growing close to old farmhouses and horseshoes nailed to barn and kitchen doors. The protection of the ash tree probably came from our Nordic ancestors and the legend of the "Yggdrasil"—the Tree of Life or World Ash, a fabulous tree which spans the measureless gap between the highest heavens and the lowest depths of hell and is cared for by the Norns, goddesses of fate and destiny. Glittering aloft and suspended from its branches hang the planets, the sun, the moon and the stars. Of course, the use of such paraphernalia is descended from the days of the witch and her evil powers—counter charms to ward off spells and keep restless spirits and demons from the door.

Superstitious beliefs die hard, but none more so than those which are the harbingers of death. In Ireland there is the popular tradition of the Banshee, an ethereal, fairy-like creature whose plaintive, mournful wail is heard before a death in the family to which it is supernaturally attached. Even nearer to home is the "Radiant Boy" of Corby Castle in Cumberland—an ancient legend revived in a work of the last century **Night Side of Nature** by Mrs Crowe. The spirit was described as a "beautiful golden haired child, clad in white" when it appeared to certain visitors at the castle. Those who saw it would soon learn whether or not they were destined for riches and success, or to die tragically. Eric Maple, that noteworthy master of the paranormal, suggests in his book **Supernatural England**; "The source of the haunting remains a mystery: the identity of the 'Golden Boy' unknown." He goes on to add that the appearance of the ghost could be accounted for by that terrible early ritual of "foundation sacrifice":

...sacrificing beautiful children in the foundations of buildings for the propitiation of demons or as a form of blood rental to the spirits of the earth.

A similar reminiscence can also be found in two lines from Shakespeare's **King John**:

There is no sure foundation set on blood.
No certain life set by other's death.

In Yorkshire the most commonly accepted portent of death manifested itself in the guise of a white rabbit. Little wonder, then, that the Rev. Wesley's family were so alarmed when a manservant saw a similar creature— sitting by the fireside in the dining room.

The last known man I could find to have witnessed such an apparition was a stone mason—a big, strapping, healthy fellow. But his name and the location of the incident were untraceable. He went with his grown-up son one moonlit night to snare sparrows in a nearby stackyard and saw the white rabbit run into a pile of brushwood in the corner. He and his son pulled away every stick but the rabbit was gone. It was impossible for the animal to have escaped, for the wall behind was new and solid. According to the son's account, his father immediately exclaimed: "I'm a dead man—a dead man!" Without another word, he went straight home to his bed and shortly afterwards died, apparently within twenty-four hours. Naturally, everyone believed that what he had seen had been sent as a warning. Some people even said that he had been fortunate, in as much as to say that the Lord had been merciful in giving him such notice for what they called his "latter end". It was never discovered what actually caused his death—it could well be that he simply died of sheer fright. But please, if **you** should be confronted by a white rabbit, don't panic. It would be wiser first to check with the neighbours to see if any of their children hasn't lost their cuddly pet bunny.

Finally, in a more sinister vein, there is one other custom I should like to mention—which concerns the campanology of the parish of Dewsbury, West Yorkshire. Since the thirteenth century, on Christmas Eve the bell-ringers of that parish have had to toll the "nine tailor" for every year of the Christian era. If this should not be dutifully and religiously performed, Satan, along with all his hordes, will assuredly attack the parish within the following twelve months. We can only hope that the tradition, if only for tradition's sake, continues for many years to come.

7:   Ursula Sontheil—alias Mother Shipton

IN JULY 1488 the most unusual child was born at Knaresborough, North Yorkshire—in, of all places, a dank cave by the river's edge. The mother's name was Agatha Sontheil, but as to that of the father, according to a reference book dated 1686, she was "begot as was the Welsh wizard Merlin, by the phantom of Apollo". It is more likely he was, as some have already suggested, a young nobleman who, rather than reveal to Agatha the true nature of his identity, claimed himself to be a spirit in disguise. Indeed, Agatha carried this belief right up until the delivery of the child, saying to the midwife: "His touch was as cold as ice or snow". Therefore the child arrived with a none too happy disposition from the very beginning, being born out of the bounds of wedlock and causing no uncertain amount of controversy when Agatha presented her for induction into the Christian Church. With some reluctance and pious indignation, the Bishop of Beverley was eventually persuaded to perform the baptism—naming the child Ursula.

When the child reached the age of two, her mother, after considerably changing her ways and seeking religious advice, entered the convent of St. Bridget in Nottingham—leaving her daughter in the charge of a caring neighbour. From here little or no information exists regarding Ursula's early life, apart from the fact that she was branded "the child of the devil" almost at the outset by the townsfolk of Knaresborough. This probably resulted from her appearance; she was reputed to have been noticeably grotesque, being quite small and dwarfish, with a hunched back. The description of her in later life is almost fearful: "Her head was long with fiery eyes, her nose of an incredible and unproportional length and encrusted with luminous pimples." But it is known that she received some form of education and became quite competent in the arts of reading and writing. Another interesting point, which would concur with her father being a "man of means", is that she never lacked money, the source of which remained, as her paternity, in anonymity.

Reaching the age of 24, Ursula decided the time was ripe for her to marry. Although her looks were highly disadvantageous for any prospective bride, she was of the mind that her having a comfortable disposition was good enough compensation for many a man. Using this as her bait, she set her cap at Tobias Shipton, originating from his namesake village, Shipton, near York, who was a carpenter by trade. Being content to be lured by the promise of prosperity, Tobias put up no struggle towards Ursula's advances and accordingly they married. Their union was never blessed with children but they lived together quite happily for a number of years before Tobias died.

The Dropping Well, Knaresborough, which has close associations with Mother Shipton. For many years, visitors and locals alike have hung a varied assortment of articles—hats, gloves, old boots and the like—to become petrified in its rich mineral waters.

It was shortly after her marriage that the first ever instance of Ursula's daunting powers of prediction was recorded. A neighbour, while preoccupied in the locquacious art of gossiping, had her washing stolen—which she bemoaned to Ursula. Promptly, without hesitation and with remarkable accuracy, she not only told the woman who the culprit was, but also where she could recover the purloined laundry. By this, and other simple predictions, she became known as "Mother Shipton", a name which was to spread far and wide and obtain her a reputation as a "cunning woman" and a "woman of foresight". Her words were soon considered oracles, advancing later into the forecasting of future national events.

This unnatural ability to make predictions or prophecies—for which she either charged a small fee, or freely dispensed, dependent upon the inquirer—seems to have been increased whenever she caused strange things to happen. This fact would, no doubt, have greatly contributed to her being considered a witch, but the majority of these "strange happenings" would appear to have been in retaliation for abuse regarding her unattractive appearance. Gaining notoriety also increased her problems, for the people in and around Knaresborough were forever prying upon her. Her privacy was constantly invaded whether she was at home or going about the town on her everyday business. Her patience finally gave way to temper, as, one day, she was subjected to a barrage of abuse with such names as "hag-face" and "devil's bastard". She decided the time had come for her to teach the townsfolk a long deserved lesson.

It so happened that a wealthy man of the district had arranged an extravagant breakfast party, many of the local dignitaries being invited. When the guests arrived they found their host had spared no expense. The tables were lavishly decorated and the fare so succulent and appealing. A mood of merriment pervaded the gathering, the air filled with the murmurings of polite and enjoyable conversation. But this atmosphere of pleasant congeniality was soon to be disrupted by a series of inexplicable events. These commenced when a rather dignified gentleman was seen, by another guest sitting at his side, to have lost his ruff—which had been mysteriously replaced by a string of sausages. The guest who had first noticed this comical transferrence thought it so amusing that he burst into fits of laughter—but not for long, as, in the midst of his frivolity, he was disquietingly halted when he learned that his hat, which had previously nestled on his head, had been just as mysteriously transformed into a pewter jug. To add even more to his injury, choose how much they tried, the jug was immovable. Sitting opposite these hapless gentlemen was a young lady, who, in a rather unbecoming fashion, started to laugh so much that she found it impossible to stop. To laugh in moderation is always considered a tonic, but to continue and still go on laughing without chance of catching one's breath is a far from enjoyable experience. Contagiously, the laughter spread around the table, one guest bellowing such great guffaws that the host, who at this point was out of the room and downstairs seeing to some minor problem, hurriedly rushed back to ascertain the reason for this uproarious revelry. When he arrived at the room door he found that his access was barred, to his amazement, by a huge pair of horns which had suddenly sprouted from his head. From whatever direction he tried to enter the room, always the horns

55

forbade his entrance. At this sight the guests grew to hysterics, many of them sliding from their chairs and rolling about on the floor in agonising convulsions of invigorated cheerfulness.

Momentarily all went silent and the tired gathering, clutching their sides and gasping for breath, became nervously apprehensive. Then they heard, as if from nowhere and much to their astonishment, a ring of laughter from a multitude of people—yet not a single soul in sight. So frightened at this were the guests that they immediately began to leave. Turning heel on their gracious host, they hurried out into the courtyard, only to be met with a volley of apples—thrown by invisible hands. Mounting their awaiting horses in a fearful panic they rode off, each, it was said, accompanied by a little, ugly, deformed crone sitting behind, the impish hags fiercely lashing the terrified beasts and making them gallop at an uncontrollable speed.

In H.L. Gee's **Folk Tales of Yorkshire**, the author draws the account to a close in the following manner:

Once safely home these people of note complained to the magistrates that they had been bewitched by Mother Shipton, who was accordingly summoned to court to account for her misdeeds. One might have expected her to plead for her life, for in the England of those days witches with far less power were burned at the stake. But Mother Shipton scorned her judges. She decided that if the people in the district worried her further she would do the same again, even worse; and at last, being tired of the whole proceedings, she shouted the mystic words, "Updraxi, call stygician Helluei," whereupon a winged dragon appeared and carried her off in a clap of thunder.

This passage only epitomizes the almost harmful damage legend can do to fact. By tagging-on some superstitious oriented anecdote, the truth eventually disappears—leaving only the superfluous element of fancy. Instead of remembering Mother Shipton as a Seer, they would prefer to think of her as a mythical character who calls up "dragons".

As a more realistic guide to Mother Shipton's prophetic powers, she once gave leave to make a famous prediction concerning the powerfully ambitious Cardinal Wolsey. After hearing of the Cardinal's intentions of moving his residence to York, she said publicly: "He should never reach the city". The news of her openly forthright statement was to come to the ears of both the Cardinal and the King, arousing their anger to such an extent that they sent the Duke of Suffolk, Lord Darcy, and another nobleman who is not named, guided by a Mr Beasly, all in disguise, to discover whether or not she had in fact said these words. They had instructions to "menace her" should she persist in voicing such claims.

The four men set out and rode to a village called Dringhouses, approximately one mile west of the city of York, where they left their horses and proceeded on foot to Mother Shipton's house. As they knocked at the door she called out to them: "Come in Mr Beasly and the three noble lords with you."

In a state of wonderment they entered, and as they did so she called each one by his full name, afterwards giving them cakes to eat and ale to drink. However, they suggested that if she knew the real purpose of their visit, she would hardly be so hospitable. "You gave out," said one, "the Cardinal should never see York".

"No," she replied, "I said he might see it but never come to it." To which he answered: "When he does come he will certainly burn thee."

Hearing this, Mother Shipton took her linen kerchief from her head, saying: "If this burn so shall I." She placed it in the flames of the fire which was burning in the grate—where it remained for a full quarter of an hour. When she retrieved the kerchief it was not so much as scorched. Once again, they appeared astounded. Another of the four men asked her what she thought of him. She answered: "The time will come, my Lord, when you shall be as low as I am, and that is low indeed."

Cardinal Wolsey, upon his arrival at Cawood Castle, some eight miles from York, ascended the tower to look at the city. Here he reaffirmed his vow that when he got to his destination he would surely burn the witch. But as he came back down the tower he was confronted by a messenger of the King, bearing a command for him to return to London with all haste. Straightway he left Cawood and was destined never to make the full journey. Taken by a violent "looseness" at Leicester, he could not continue further— he died shortly afterwards, fulfilling the prophecy.

Perhaps one of the longest prefigurements she made, which was initially prepared for the Abbot of Beverley, takes in almost every major historical event between the sixteenth and seventeenth centuries—all coming to fruition long after her death in the 1560s. The original manuscript of this epic, saga-like string of predictions is purported to be in the custody of a local noble family—but I could find no reference to the name of this custodian in any local or general history book. This is the way in which Mother Shipton presented her revelations to the good Abbot (the predictions are taken from Shirley MacLean's booklet, **Mother Shipton and her Prophecies, Past Present and Future,** and also included are their respective interpretations):

*For a sweet pious Prince make room
And in each Kirk prepare a broom
For this Prince that never shall be born
Shall make the shaven heads forlorn.*

(The Prince she refers to became King Edward VI, his mother, Lady Jane Seymour, dying as a direct result of the hazardous child-birth— a crude form of caesarean section. The "shaven heads" are presumed to be the clergy, cast adrift by the Reformation, believed to be in excess of 10,000—beginning at the commencement of Edward's reign.)

*Then shall Commons rise in arms,
And women's malice cause much harm.
O deadly Pride! O hateful strife!
Brothers to seek each other's life,
Ambition shall so deadly spread,
The Griffin fierce shall lose his head,
Soon after shall the Lion die,
And mildness usher cruelty.*

(The people of England were in a dire state at this time, suffering badly with no indication of assistance. This was when Somerset (the Protector) decided to try and find some remedy by setting up a commission to hear the people's plaints. The gentry were very much against the scheme, so much so that their violent opposition became apparent when they labelled Somerset's idea arbitrary and illegal. But the commoners were impatient for repeal, and were ready to rise up in revolt to bring about a speedier change. Indeed, an uprising did emerge in certain parts of the country, and would have spread but for the intervention of the Earl of Warwick, along with 6,000 men at arms, who was called on to quell all signs of rebellion. Many of the leaders of the insurrection were hanged, an act which partially restored an unsettled peace. The "woman's malice" is allegorically aligned to the marriage of Catherine Parr with Lord Seymour—Seymour hoping to gain power by the coupling.)

A virtuous lady then shall die
For being raised up too high -
Her death shall cause another's joy,
Who will the kingdom much annoy.

(The "virtuous lady" was undoubtedly Lady Jane Grey, beheaded at the tender age of sixteen for assuming the title of queen.)

Alecto next assumes the crown;
And mitres shall rise, and heads fall down
And streams of blood run Smithfield down,
England shall join in league with Spain,
Which some to hinder strive in vain.
Alecto then from Life retire,
And Pontifical Priest expire.

(The "Alecto") of the prophecy was Queen Mary, who is supposed to have rejoiced at the death of Lady Jane Grey; for it was her intention to restore popery—with which also came the hated persecutions in the name of faith. Countless martyrs were burned at Smithfield in Mary's reign, under the supervision of Bishop Boner and Dr Storey, Dean of St. Pauls. Mary wished to marry Phillip of Spain, but the people did not take kindly to the idea of a foreign king, causing her popularity to waver. Her reign was comparatively short, a little over five-years—she died of dropsy. The "Pontifical Priest" was Cardinal Cole, who died within hours of Mary.)

First being dead and gone
A maiden queen shall reign anon.
The maiden Queen full many a year
Shall England's warlike sceptre bear.
Those who sighed then shall sing,
And the bells shall changes ring.
The Papal power shall bear no sway,
And Rome's trash shall hence be swept away.
The Locusts from the Seven hills,
This English rose shall seek to kill-
And the Western monarch's wooden horses
Shall be destroyed by Drake's forces.

(Elizabeth was the "maiden queen" who came to the throne in 1558 at the age of twenty-five. Her reign was full and long, lasting more than forty years—and remaining "maiden". During this time the Queen made many new laws. After her accession a Parliament began at Westminster —through which the "bells shall changes ring"—the laws of Henry VIII against the See of Rome being renewed, along with those of Edward VI in favour of the Protestants. Queen Mary's laws against them were also rebuilt. The last two lines refer to the Armada, thought to be invincible, and Drake's triumphant victory.)

Great London's triumphant spire,
Shall be consumed with flames of fire-
More wonders yet! A widowed Queen,
In England shall be headless seen,
The harp shall give a better sound;
An Earl without a head be found.
Soon after shall the English Rose,
Unto a male her place dispose.

(The first two lines denote the destruction by fire in 1561 of St. Paul's steeple. The "widowed Queen" was Mary, Queen of Scots, the mother of King James, who was beheaded at Fotheringay Castle by order of Elizabeth. The harp refers to Ireland, where, for once, the situation was notably more peaceful. As to the "Earl", this was Essex, one time Governor of Ireland, who, although a firm favourite of both the Queen and the people, was not above beheading. When Elizabeth, the "English Rose", died with no heirs, the right and title of the crown came to James VI of Scotland, James I of England.)

The Northern Lion o'er the Tweed,
The maiden Queen shall next succeed,
And join in one, two mighty states—
Then shall Janus shut his gates.

(Again, this pertains to James' inheritance of the English crown— and to him having to come over the Tweed to take up his new residence in London. Thus, the "two mighty states" were joined as one. Her reference to Janus shutting his gates— Janus being a heathen god who had a temple in Rome, the gates of which were only shut in times of peace— was alluding to the peaceful reign of James I.):

Mars shall yield to Mercury,
All things tend to prosperity.
Hell's power by a fatal blow,
Shall seek the land to overthrow
Which by mistake shall be reversed,
And heads from shoulders be dispersed.

(Here, the inference is clearly the Gunpowder Plot, designed to be rid of both the King and Parliament in one almighty bang—resulting in the execution of the plotters. A Yorkshireman by the name of Guy Fawkes who lived at Scotton was the main leader of the conspirators.)

The British Olive next shall twine,
In marriage with the German Vine.
The ninth to Death his powers shall yield,
Death conquers all—he wins the Field.

(This concerns the marriage of James' daughter, Lady Elizabeth, to Prince Frederick of Germany on the 14th February, 1602. The "ninth" is Prince Henry, son of the King, who, had he lived, would have become Henry IX—he died in 1625.)

This Crown then fits the White King's
   head.
Who with Lilies soon shall wed.
Then shall a peasant's bloody knife,
Deprive a great man of his Life.

(The "White King" was Charles I, called this for one of two reasons, firstly because of his purity and uprightness. The second is more appropriate in that at his Coronation his entire ensemble was white. He married Lady Henrietta Maria, daughter of Henry IV of France—the

59

lily of the prophecy. As to the "peasant", he is thought to have been the officer named Feton who deprived the Duke of Buckingham of his life while serving in the Duke's army. For his crime, he was hanged in chains at Portsmouth in 1627.)

Forth from the North shall mischief blow
And English Hob shall add hereto
For now the Council great assemble,
And make both great and small to
    tremble.

(This is supposed to indicate the troubles in Scotland in 1630, to the war, rebellion and defeat of Charles' army at Newburn. Parliament was the 'Council' - which voted down episcopacy in favour of presbytory.):

Mars shall rage as if he were wood;
And earth shall be drunken with blood-
The North shall rue its wondrous sore,
But the South shall rue it evermore.
When war shall begin in the Spring;
Much woe to England it will bring;
Then shall the ladies cry, "Well-a-day,
That ere we lived to see this day."
Then best for them that have the least
And worst for them that have the most
But tell what's next; oh! cruel fate,
A King made martyr at his gate.
The White King then "oh grief to see"
By wicked hands he martyred be.

(Unquestionably this was the Civil War, which began one spring morning in 1642 at Edge Hill, the misery culminating in the beheading of King Charles on 30th January, 1649.)

The White King dead, the Wolf shall then
With blood usurp the Lion's den.

(With Charles dead, the Wolf—Oliver Cromwell—mercilessly clawed his way through any and every Royalist to take control of the "Lion's den", becoming the Lord Protector and sole government.)

But death shall snatch him hence away:
Confusion shall awhile bear sway;
Till fate to England shall restore
A King to reign as heretofore-
Who mercy, and justice likewise
Shall in this Empire exercise,-

(This very descriptive passage covering the end of Cromwell is taken from some rather ancient material housed at the British Library: "Very remarkable was the day on which the Protector, Cromwell died, being September 3rd, 1658, wherein the wind was so violent, that it overthrew many houses, tore up many trees by the roots, tumbled down chimneys and unroofed barns and stables; but, as it is a very ill wind that blows none good, so with all the hurt this wind did, it made recompense to some folks who had lost their estates in the Civil Wars, by blowing this Oliver away." At the death of Cromwell, Charles II came to the throne on the 29th May, 1660, and restored the Commonwealth.)

60

Triumphant Death rides London through,
And men on tops of houses go.

(Accountable by the great Plague which visited its wrath on London in 1665—an epidemic to be unrivalled. The last line was fulfilled by the devastating "Fire of London" which raged continually through the 2nd, 3rd and 4th of September, 1666, causing so many buildings to be burned to the ground that men, in the ruins, walked on the tops of houses.)

Towards the end of making this spectacular composition of mainly stanzaic versifications of Homeric proportions, Mother Shipton commented:

Unhappy is he that lives to see these days,
But happy the dead, Shipton's wife says.

This was a clear indication to the Abbot that she did not wish to continue further. But he was not content, and, wishing to hear more of her wonderful, portentuous prose, began to try and cajole the words from her. With some reluctance, she replied:

Let this suffice, the night comes on,
You must depart - so now begone__
Apollo does forbid my rhymes;
For to unveil succeeding times.

Unable to get her to speak again, the Abbot took his leave of Mother Shipton with the intention of deciphering the words of the prodigious sibyl. This proved to be his final visit to the old woman for she died shortly afterwards. Not surprisingly, Mother Shipton even foretold the exact date of her own death in 1561, at a time when as much as two-thirds of this epic prophecy had not yet come to pass.

It has never been discovered as to how these inspirational forewarnings came to her—whether in dreams at the dead of night, or sudden thoughts into her waking consciousness. There are no reports to suggest that she ever made use of "divinatory forecasting aids" like astrology, cards or the crystal ball. Therefore, we can only assume that she was the beholder of a remarkable, natural, yet unnatural gift.

She was buried in unconsecrated ground, a tradition more normally reserved for criminals, suicides and witches. The actual site is commonly believed to be between Shipton Road and Rawcliffe Lane on the outskirts of York. A stone was laid to mark the spot, but, for the sake of conservation, was moved in later years for safe-keeping to the Yorkshire Museum in York. Alas, for some uncanny reason, the stone, which took the form of a small statuette, cannot be traced. But, although little recompense, the epitaph it bore has been recorded for posterity:

Here lies she who never ly'd,
Whose skill has so often been try'd,
Her prophecies shall still survive,
And ever keep her name alive.

Before going on to mention some of her even further reaching premonitions, some extending into the twentieth century—almost five-hundred years after her birth—there was one unusual prediction of hers entitled "The Mother Shipton Prophecy", first published in 1548 and reissued in 1641, of which the last two lines were long considered to be of a different authorship. Indeed, it so happened that they had been added by some prankish students from the southern regions in the nineteenth-century:

Over a wild and stormy sea
Shall a noble sail
Who to find will not fail
A new and fair countree,
From whence he shall bring
A herb and a root
That all men shall suit
And please both the ploughman and King;
And let them take no more than measure.
Both shall have the even pleasure.

The world then to an end shall come
In Eighteen Hundred and Eighty one.

The first ten lines can readily be associated with Sir Walter Raleigh and his discovery of America, from where he brought the tobacco leaf and the potato—but as to the last two lines, these were proved, as I have already stated, to have been bogus.

According to Eric Maple's book **Supernatural England**, a similar Mother Shipton apocalyptic warning of an equally dubious nature must have been released in the 1840s. During 1842, to be more precise, on the 17th March, vast numbers of people, under the misapprehension that the end of London was nigh, disposed of all their belongings at rock-bottom prices—then waited in vain for the promised Armageddon. Needless-to-say, London is still with us; but this would illustrate just how convinced many people were, and still are, of the exactitude so often displayed in the words of Mother Shipton.

Contrary to the capers of 1842 and 1881, here is a more demonstrative compilation of what she saw in the fates for "modern man", taken from a small booklet, **Mother Shipton and her Prophecies, Past, Present and Future,** written by Mrs Shirley MacLean, the Managing Director of the Dropping Well Estate at Knaresborough. She has gone to considerable pains to present as much factual evidence as possible on such a fascinating subject in so small a publication. But she gave me a cautionary warning when she so courteously granted me permission to use and quote from that same booklet. Although Mother Shipton's prophecies of an historical connotation are to be considered authentic, the following, which mainly appeared in **Blackwood's Journal,** could well have been a contrivance of some latter-day Mother Shipton. However, until such time as this theory is given ratification, if ever at all, we shall accept them as being legitimate:

A house of glass shall come to pass   (Crystal Palace)
In England, but alas!
War will follow with the work,   (Crimean War)
In the land of the Pagan and Turk
And state and state in fierce strife,
Will seek each other's life
But when the North shall divide the South
An eagle shall build in the lion's mouth.   (American Civil War)

ron in the water shall float   (Modern boats)
As easy as a wooden boat;
Gold shall be found, and found
In a land that's not now known.   (America)
Fire and water shall more wonders do
England shall at last admit a Jew;   (Thought to be Disraeli)
The Jew that was held in scorn
Shall of a Christian be born and born.

Around the world thoughts shall fly
In a twinkling of an eye.   (Radio satellite)

Carriages without horses shall go,   (Modern transport)
And accidents fill the world with woe.
Primrose Hill in London shall be   (In the time of Mother Shipton,
And in its centre a Bishop's See.   Primrose Hill would have been two miles
                    from the centre of London—now
           it is almost in the middle of the city.)
Through hills men shall ride
And no horse or ass by their side   (Mont Blanc Tunnel)
Under water men shall walk,
Shall ride, shall sleep, shall talk;   (Submarines)
In the air men shall be seen
In white, in black, and in green.   (Aeroplanes)
Men shall walk over rivers and under rivers. (Mersey Tunnel, etc.)
All England's sons that plough the land,
Shall be seen book in hand;   (Education for all
Learning shall so ebb and flow,   The age of leisure following
The poor shall most wisdom know.   the silicon revolution.)

    With further reference to these "latter-day Mother Shipton's", a section of Mrs MacLean's booklet is dedicated to an assortment of predictions that have been sent to her from various people via the Estate—one of whom, a lady from Australia, actually believes herself to be a reincarnation of the Yorkshire prophetess. But this lady should not be considered in a class of her own; another lady confesses that she cannot under normal circumstances write "ordinary poetry". Yet it is somehow different when she is inspired by Mother Shipton, who, in some unexplained way, tells her what to write—which she feels obligated to proclaim to the world. Mrs MacLean wisely offers no allegorical meaning to these predictions when introducing them, commenting thus: "Perhaps the people who now seek to prophesy in her style do so more for gain, or may it be, as some correspondents suggest, Mother Shipton who is striving to influence present day events through mediums. This idea is so fraught with problems, it is hard to judge the merits, but we leave it to the reader to decipher the wisdom or otherwise of the various verses set out below." Likewise, I offer two of the examples, under the same terms of condition:

Example I

When waters-mede is bally-brook
And habitat forsook

Shalt lair and fox part company
And History be afoot.
When ditch and dyke are thus unite
Beyond the power of man,
Shall lie beneath the surface
The man-made dam.

Example II.

The stars will tell you when the "hour" is come;
When day and night merge as one
And man and beast alike
Search for the warming sun.

I can well understand some authors in the past to have disputed the "talents" of Mother Shipton—but to deny her very existence, as some have, H.L. Gee being amongst them, is quite ridiculous. There is official documented evidence available which states to the contrary. Ursula Sontheil/Seathiel/Southeil/Sondial, as she is named in various records, was indisputably a fifteenth to sixteenth-century inhabitant of Knaresborough.

For many years, the Dropping Well, Wishing Well and Mother Shipton's Cave have been visited by many thousands of people from almost every country the world over—all of them ever curious and ever seeking a brief glimpse into the past of this veritable Cassandra of the North, whose forecasting powers, whether they were founded in heaven or hell, have never been rivalled before or since.

Artist's impression of the Yorkshire prophetess, Mother Shipton, seated in the cave where she is purported to have been born—a clap of thunder heralding the birth of this far seeing oracle of the sixteenth-century.